VIOLENCE
WITHOUT GOD

VIOLENCE WITHOUT GOD

The rhetorical despair of twentieth-century writers

JOYCE WEXLER

Bloomsbury Academic
An imprint of Bloomsbury Publishing Inc

B L O O M S B U R Y
NEW YORK · LONDON · OXFORD · NEW DELHI · SYDNEY

Bloomsbury Academic
An imprint of Bloomsbury Publishing Inc

1385 Broadway	50 Bedford Square
New York	London
NY 10018	WC1B 3DP
USA	UK

www.bloomsbury.com

BLOOMSBURY and the Diana logo are trademarks of Bloomsbury Publishing Plc

First published 2017

Library of Congress Cataloging-in-Publication Data
Names: Wexler, Joyce Piell, 1947- author.
Title: Violence without God : the rhetorical despair of twentieth-century writers / Joyce Wexler.
Description: New York : Bloomsbury Academic, 2016. | Includes bibliographical references and index.
Identifiers: LCCN 2016020328 (print) | LCCN 2016039152 (ebook) | ISBN 9781501325298 (hardback) | ISBN 9781501325311 (ePub) | ISBN 9781501325304 (ePDF)
Subjects: LCSH: Violence in literature. | Atrocities in literature. | Despair in literature. | Rhetoric and psychology. | Authors–20th century–Psychology. | Authors–21st century–Psychology. | Literature, Modern–20th century–History and criticism. | Literature, Modern–21st century–History and criticism. | BISAC: LITERARY CRITICISM / General. | LITERARY CRITICISM / Semiotics & Theory.
Classification: LCC PN56.V53 W49 2016 (print) | LCC PN56.V53 (ebook) | DDC 809/.933552–dc23
LC record available at https://lccn.loc.gov/2016020328

ISBN:	HB:	978-1-5013-2529-8
	PB:	978-1-5013-2528-1
	ePub:	978-1-5013-2531-1
	ePDF:	978-1-5013-2530-4

Cover design: Eleanor Rose
Cover image © akg-images/DACS 2016

Typeset by Integra Software Services Pvt. Ltd.
Printed and bound in the United States of America

To my loving family, without whom nothing would have been written

CONTENTS

ACKNOWLEDGMENTS

This is an opportunity to thank many people. The following list is not complete, but it is a start: Bloomsbury's anonymous readers whose suggestions sharpened my argument; the members of the Joseph Conrad Society, the D. H. Lawrence Society, and the T. S. Eliot Society who responded to earlier versions of several chapters; the staff of the Neue Gallerie in New York City for early access to the exhibits in 2002; graduate and undergraduate students at Loyola University Chicago; my colleagues in the English department and throughout the University. I am also grateful to Samuel Hynes and Kevin J. H. Dettmar for their encouragement early in my career.

I would also like to acknowledge permission to include revised versions of the following essays:

"Writing About Violence in a Secular Age: Conrad's Solution," *College Literature* 39 (2012): 98–109.

"T. S. Eliot's Expressionist Angst." In *T. S. Eliot, France, and the Mind of Europe*. Ed. Jayme Stayer. Newcastle upon Tyne, UK: Cambridge Scholars Publishing, 2015. 214–30.

"Violence and Laughter in *Women in Love*," *D. H. Lawrence Review* 36 (2011): 56–71 and in *Great War Modernism*. Ed. Nanette Norris. Madison: Fairleigh Dickinson University Press, 2016.

"The German Detour from *Ulysses* to Magic Realism," *Modern Language Quarterly* 70 (2009): 245–68.

"Falling Towers: *The Waste Land* and September 11, 2001." In *The Waste Land at 90: A Retrospective.* Ed. Joe Moffett. Amsterdam, Netherlands: Rodopi, 2011. 217–25.

For permission to publish the following images:

Wassily Kandinsky, *Reiter:*© 2016 Artists Rights Society (ARS), New York

Carlo Carrá, *Reiter*: © 2016 Artists Rights Society (ARS), New York/SIAE, Rome

Otto Dix, *Zwei Kinder*: © 2016 Artists Rights Society (ARS), New York/VG Bild-Kunst, Bonn

George Schrimpf, *Auf der Treppe/Am Abend*: © 2016 Artists Rights Society (ARS), New York/VG Bild-Kunst, Bonn

George Grosz, *Mann und Frau*: VAGA

For providing the following images:

AKG: for George Schrimpf *Auf der Treppe/Am Abend* and George Grosz, *Mann und Frau.*

Musées royaux des Beaux-Arts de Belgique: for Otto Dix, *Zwei Kinder*

Scala: for Carlo Carrá, *Reiter*

Introduction:
The problem

As twentieth-century writers confronted the political violence of their time, they were overcome by rhetorical despair. Unimaginable events seemed as inexpressible as nightmares. In Joseph Conrad's *Heart of Darkness*, Marlow says that his contact with colonialism is "like a weary pilgrimage amongst hints for nightmares."[1] In James Joyce's *Ulysses*, Stephen Dedalus uses the same metaphor: "History...is a nightmare from which I am trying to awake."[2] Halfway through the century, Gabriel García Márquez wrote a newspaper article regarding the obstacles to writing about "the nightmare of violence" (*la pesadilla de la violencia*) in Colombia's civil wars.[3] In Salman Rushdie's *Midnight's Children*, Saleem says that the Partition of India in 1947 was a time when "myths, nightmares, fantasies were in the air."[4] Unspeakable violence left writers speechless. In 1923, T. S. Eliot doubted that anyone could

---

[1] Joseph Conrad, *Heart of Darkness*, 4th edn, ed. Paul B. Armstrong (New York: W. W. Norton, 2006), 14.
[2] James Joyce, *Ulysses*, ed. Hans Walter Gabler (New York: Vintage Books, 1986), 28.
[3] Gabriel García Márquez, "Dos o tres cosas sobre 'la novela de la violencia,'" in *De Europa y América, Obra periodística 3 (1955–1960)* (Barcelona: Mondadori, 1992), 649.
[4] Salman Rushdie, *Midnight's Children* (New York: Random House, 2006), 123.

create art about "the immense panorama of futility and anarchy which is contemporary history."[5] Speaking for the next generation, Theodor Adorno remarked that writing poetry after Auschwitz was barbaric.[6] At the end of the century, W. G. Sebald observed that the destruction in the Second World War "pales when described in … stereotypical phrases."[7] All these writers knew that the atrocities of the century had to be represented, but they saw that this was a daunting responsibility.

Although the writers' statements imply that the violence of the twentieth century was unprecedented, the historical record of heinous acts is long and vicious. What made writing about twentieth-century violence so difficult was that it occurred in a secular age. I take this phrase from the title of Charles Taylor's sweeping intellectual history of the West, *A Secular Age* (2007). Taylor develops a concept of "secularity" in opposition to the common understanding of secularism as the removal of religion from personal and public life.[8] He defines secularity not as the absence of religion but as the absence of a consensus of belief. Taylor traces the gradual transition "from a society in which it was virtually impossible not to believe in God, to one in which faith, even for the staunchest believer, is one human possibility

---

[5] T. S. Eliot, "*Ulysses*, Order, and Myth," in *Selected Prose of T. S. Eliot*, ed. Frank Kermode (New York: Harcourt Brace Jovanovich, 1975), 177.

[6] Theodor Adorno, "Cultural Criticism and Society," in *Prisms*, trans. Samuel and Shierry Weber (Cambridge, MA: MIT Press, 1967), 34.

[7] W. G. Sebald, *On the Natural History of Destruction*, trans. Anthea Bell (New York: Random House, 2003), 25.

[8] See Colin Jager, "Romanticism/Secularization/Secularism," *Literature Compass* 5 (2008): 799. Jager's summary of current conceptions of secularism demonstrates how influential Taylor's views have been. Jager states that there is "widespread agreement" that "'The Religious' is not the opposite of 'The Secular.'" The two concepts are interdependent, and "religion appears as marked, set against the neutral or unmarked background of the secular."

among others."[9] Once the religious consensus fell apart, a proliferation of beliefs, both religious and nonreligious, weakened all of them. The result was a "mutual fragilization of all the different views," a new sense of "the fragility of any particular formula or solution, whether believing or unbelieving" (303). Taylor observes that despite "widespread agreement that something was missing, there was no consensus on what it was" (400). This narrative of a lost consensus is based on a comprehensive idea of religion as belief in something "beyond" rather than "within" human life (15). Taylor explains: "So 'religion' for our purposes can be defined in terms of 'transcendence', . . . the sense that there is some good higher than, beyond human flourishing" (20). Throughout centuries of religious controversy, much of it violent, the assumption that divine power existed was unchallenged. By the late nineteenth century, however, the demise of axiomatic belief in transcendence resulted in a plethora of options. None of them had the unifying force of belief in God. The meaning of violence could no longer be grounded in a transcendent order.

In the past, communal beliefs had justified or condemned the most horrific acts, but the "sad record of continuing violence" causes Taylor to ask, "Why is it still with us? Why are we still perpetuating it ourselves?" (691). "One part of the answer," he proposes, is that "the more minimalist rules which are supposed to guarantee harmony are inherently morally instable" (691). While the extreme violence of the twentieth century had many causes, Taylor suggests that at least one factor was the instability of meaning.

---

[9] Charles Taylor, *A Secular Age* (Cambridge, MA: Belknap Press of Harvard University Press, 2007), 3.

Taylor's concept of secularity provides a cultural context for the dilemma that writers faced. To write about violence is to give it a meaning. A dead body does not explain itself, and the narrative of the suicide bomber is not the story of the child killed in the blast. Derek Walcott's 1962 poem, "A Far Cry from Africa," names some of the obstacles to representing violence:

> Only the worm, colonel of carrion, cries:
> "Waste no compassion on these separate dead!"
> Statistics justify and scholars seize
> The salients of colonial policy.
> What is that to the white child hacked in bed?
> To savages, expendable as Jews?[10]

The speaker expresses his ethical stance negatively: only a worm could be indifferent to the "separate dead," whether the victim is white or black, African or European. Every victim deserves compassion, and violence should not be measured by its magnitude or its purpose. Neither "statistics" nor "policy" matters to victims. The deaths of a single white child, savages, and Jews are equally significant. Nevertheless, the duty to recognize each victim conflicts with the most basic attempt to represent violence by counting the dead: "Statistics justify." As Walcott suggests, neither the number of victims nor the motive for killing determines the enormity of the act. If even raw numbers insert victims into a tendentious discourse, how can violence be made known?

---

[10] Derek Walcott, *Collected Poems: 1948–1984* (New York: Farrar, Straus & Giroux, 1986), 17.

Some of the most influential authors of the period tried to answer this question. While their formal innovations are usually attributed to their interest in conveying subjective experience, particularly in the first half of the century, new forms also allowed writers to represent contemporary events. Although formal innovation has been regarded as an evasion of social responsibility, it has also been defended as a sign of social commitment. Between the world wars, for example, the demand for socialist realism was countered by the assertion that revolutionary art had a revolutionary political impact.[11] It is no longer uncommon to find political meaning in new forms, yet the social value of symbolism is still questioned. Michael Levenson traces such doubts to the late nineteenth-century aim of expressing immaterial reality:

On one side, symbolist poets, critics, and dramatists repudiated the coarse materiality of everyday social life, progressive or reactionary; on the other side, they pursued an aesthetic vision—

---

[11] See Janice Ho, "The Crisis of Liberalism and the Politics of Modernism," *Literature Compass* 8 (2011): 47–65. Ho summarizes the main arguments about the "politics of modernist aesthetics and the ideological content of modernist form" (48). Taking Georg Lukács's 1934 indictment of Expressionism as a "synecdoche of modernist art in general" (52), she explains that "in their privileging of the realm of subjective perception, Expressionist works of art tended to present a world abstracted from the concrete particularities and causal movements of history" (51). Lukács "contrasts the critical capacities of realism against the impoverished nihilism of modernism" and lists the "aesthetic devices" of modernism that turn away from reality: "its excessive formalism, its solipsistic presentation of mental life, its interest in the psycho-pathological, its lack of verisimilitude" (52). In contrast, Theodor Adorno defends modernism's social commitment, claiming that its formal qualities are "progressive and revolutionary" (52). Adorno argues that art must reveal "'whatever is veiled by the empirical form assumed by reality'" (53) and that aesthetic form "is the very element that confers upon the artwork a measure of critical independence from the status quo" (53). Later, Fredric Jameson "pioneered a new method of reading, the 'hermeneutics of suspicion', by which critics would interpret aesthetic form in terms of the ideologies that were implicitly buried within" (57).

the "ideal" or "super-sensible" world—available only to initiates. The symbolist salon with its select company and its obscure ceremonies may seem to stand as far as possible from political engagement.[12]

In contrast, Taylor regards symbolic representation as an authentic response to violence in a secular period. He argues that the choice between the *what* of realism and the *why* of symbolism was skewed by the breakdown of religious consensus. Secularity pushed writers toward symbolic forms:

> Where before the languages of theology and metaphysics confidently mapped out the domain of the deeper, the "invisible", now the thought is that these domains can only be made indirectly accessible through a language of "symbols".[13]

Although the languages of theology and metaphysics also employ symbolism, belief systems constrain the meaning of their symbols. For example, in the Eucharist, the symbolic meaning of bread and wine is fixed by doctrine, but outside this context bread and wine can symbolize many other things. The visible world is available for diverse symbolic meanings. As Taylor points out, the formal consequence of the proliferation of beliefs in a secular period was that symbolic meaning became radically indeterminate: "where formerly poetic language [symbols] could rely on certain publicly available orders of meaning, it now has to consist in a language of articulated sensibility" (353). Once "publicly available orders of meaning" were replaced by

---

[12] Michael Levenson, *Modernism* (New Haven: Yale University Press, 2011), 13.
[13] Taylor, *A Secular Age*, 357.

"a language of articulated sensibility," symbolism changed. Taylor provides a cultural explanation for this change: in the absence of communal beliefs, symbolism evoked individual meanings.

Writers had to balance the value of describing actual events against the danger of appearing to explain them. Absorbing the aesthetic ideas of their time, the writers I discuss understood this dilemma as a choice between realism and symbolism. While realism refers to particular empirical events, symbolism provides a structure of substitution that implies connections and explanations beyond the immediate referent. Symbolism and other strategies allowed writers to represent violence without imposing a specific meaning on events or claiming to explain them.[14] The indeterminate forms of twentieth-century writing are not turning away from contemporary events but representing the enormity of extreme experience after the loss of communal belief.

The advantage of symbolism is that it accommodates many meanings, but this became its Achilles heel. After the First World War, the ambiguity of idiosyncratic symbols began to count as a liability. Taylor argues that the war drained symbolism of its spiritual exuberance, because "the trauma could create a sense of uncertainty, of disbelief and even cynicism. The idea could be accredited that there is no morally credible publicly established order, the diametrical opposite of the previously established synthesis" (408). Symbolism

---

[14] See Pericles Lewis, *Religious Experience and the Modernist Novel* (Cambridge: Cambridge University Press, 2010), 25. Lewis argues that the modernist generation's "quest for a modern form of the 'secular sacred' underwrote many of their experiments with form and technique; in particular, they sought the means to combine naturalistic descriptions of the visible world, such as those that the great realist novelists of the nineteenth century had offered, with spiritual insight of the kind found in the symbolist poets. If God died in the nineteenth century, he had an active afterlife in the twentieth."

produced too many meanings. Consensus is never more important than when violence occurs, but the collapse of the previous moral order made communal belief unattainable. Although the ethical imperative to bear witness to violence continued, authors sacrificed the clarity of realism for the truth of uncertainty.

As the ubiquity of religious belief ended, the post-Enlightenment philosophy of Sensationism prevented a new consensus from forming. Drawing on Taylor's earlier book, *Sources of the Self: Making of the Modern Identity* (1990), the historian Yuval Noah Harari argues that the rise of Sensationism exacerbated the difficulty of representing violence. In *The Ultimate Experience: Battlefield Revelations and the Making of Modern War Culture, 1450–2000* (2008), Harari shows how Sensationism changed soldiers' accounts of combat. By studying military memoirs from the Renaissance to the present, he locates a turning point in the middle of the eighteenth century.[15] Before then, soldiers recorded what happened and what they did. Sensationism, however, shifted the foundation of knowledge from sensory perception to emotional response:

Feeling became synonymous with knowing, and to this day Westerners often say "I feel" when they actually mean "I think." As Charles Taylor explains, though reason could still guide and

---

[15] Yuval Noah Harari, *The Ultimate Experience: Battlefield Revelations and the Making of Modern War Culture, 1450–2000* (Hampshire: Palgrave Macmillan, 2008), 135–36. Harari identifies the French and British proponents of Sensationism and explains that "Sensationist philosophers refrained from adopting materialist views and from denying the existence of immaterial souls or minds. However, they agreed with La Mettrie that all ideas and all knowledge are the product of bodily sensations. There is nothing in the mind that did not originate in some sensation or the other. They thereby subordinated minds and souls to bodies."

correct feelings when they deviated from the right path, feelings yielded crucial insights that reason could never produce by itself. (138)

As a result, each person's inner experience was a distinct source of truth. This view replaced the Enlightenment's trust in the validity of empirical observations that could be corroborated by others. Events and acts were less important than how a person felt. Since individual feeling could not be verified or disputed, there was no basis for agreement. When soldiers tried to write about their extreme experiences, they discovered that their feelings were impossible to describe.

Harari argues that combat is indescribable for the same reasons that the eighteenth century considered the sublime inexpressible: only those who have faced an overwhelming force can know how it feels. Although *sublime* has become a synonym for *superb*, in the eighteenth century Edmund Burke defined the sublime as a force to be feared, as gods had been feared. Sources of the sublime are "pain, and danger, that is to say, whatever is in any sort terrible."[16] The sublime is "the strongest emotion which the mind is capable of feeling," because "the torments which we may be made to suffer" have a greater effect on the mind and body than any pleasure (59). Burke's example of the sublime is the ocean, which evokes terror and astonishment (97–98); Harari's example is war. Warfare provides the essential conditions of the sublime in abundance: "It is particularly noteworthy that Burke, Kant, and Schiller grounded the sublime in the sense of self-preservation,

---

[16] Edmund Burke, *A Philosophical Enquiry into the Origin of our Ideas of the Sublime and Beautiful*, 2nd edn. (London: R. & J. Dodsley, 1759, ECCO release 11/01/2004), 58.

arguing that terror and fear of death are at the bottom of the sublime experience."[17] The sublime is dreaded, yet people who survive it are transformed. They believe that they know what is true.

Harari emphasizes that Burke's idea of the sublime does not depend on belief in God:

> The sublime was the Romantic counterpart of religious revelation. It was, however, secular in essence, for it depended on encounters with immanent reality in the shape of mountains or storms, rather than on encounters with a transcendental reality. The sublime may be seen as the vacuum left in the field of human knowledge once the Enlightenment removed God from the scene. (154–55)

Though secular, the sublime is as compelling as a religious revelation. Unlike a religious epiphany, however, the sublime leads to competing truths that perpetuate the absence of communal belief that Taylor observes. Harari notes, "Though the truths revealed by sublime epiphanies were diverse, the common assumption was that a truth revealed in such a manner was superior to truths which were reached by any other means" (154). Those who confront the sublime are initiates, but they do not form a community of belief. Each person's revelation is absolute; it is incommunicable and incontrovertible.

Harari introduces the term "flesh-witnessing" to distinguish Sensationism from empiricism. He takes the term from a French veteran of the First World War who said that a man "who has not understood *with his flesh* cannot talk to you about it."[18] Whereas

---

[17] Harari, *Ultimate Experience*, 155.
[18] Yuval Noah Harari, "Scholars, Eyewitnesses, and Flesh-Witnesses of War: A Tense Relationship," *Partial Answers* 7 (2009): 215.

eyewitness reports provide information that can be communicated to others, the knowledge of the flesh-witness can never be known by anyone else. Since feelings of terror and awe are incommunicable, the violence of war became inexpressible:

> Henceforth, a central tenet of the new stories of war was that those who did not undergo the key experiences of war cannot understand these experiences and cannot understand war in general.
>
> Two stock expressions repeat themselves in Romantic memoirs: "It is impossible to describe it" and "You had to undergo the experience yourself in order to understand it."[19]

Harari's survey of nonliterary representations of warfare extends Taylor's claims about secularity: the loss of consensus weakened all beliefs, and the primacy of individual feeling as a source of knowledge made extreme experience seem inexpressible. From this perspective, the soldier is silent because civilians are incapable of understanding any account of his experience, not because he is incapable of remembering or confronting it.

After the Second World War, the difficulty of describing violence was inescapable. Among the explanations that were proposed, postmodernism and trauma theory overlap with Taylor and Harari on some but not all points. In "Pluralism in Postmodern Perspective," for example, Ihab Hassan identifies a "catena of postmodern features" of the literary response to the war.[20] Although Hassan locates these

---

[19] Harari, *Ultimate Experience*, 232.

[20] Ihab Hassan, "Pluralism in Postmodern Perspective," in *The Postmodern Turn: Essays in Postmodern Theory and Culture* (Columbus: Ohio State University Press, 1987), 168.

features in mid-century literature, he admits that they do not "serve to distinguish postmodernism from modernism" (173). He perceives that the "ultimate opprobrium is 'totalization'—any synthesis whatever, social, epistemic, even poetic" (168). Distrust of totalizing narratives and indeterminacy of meaning are qualities that Taylor observes at the turn of the century. Like Taylor, Hassan argues that the breakdown in consensus leads to formal innovation: "all the evasions of our knowledge and actions thrive on the absence of consensual beliefs, an absence that also energizes our tempers, our wills. This is our postmodern condition" (182). Like Harari, Hassan associates violence with the sublime, suggesting that postmodernism resembles the "Kantian Sublime" in its awareness of the "unpresentable," the "unrepresentable" (169). In "The Literature of Silence," Hassan also attributes new literary forms to extreme violence:

> The violence I associate with the new literature is obviously of a special kind; it presupposes Dachau and Hiroshima but is not necessarily limited by them. It is absurd in the sense that no meaning or value can be assigned to it. Its function is to turn men into things; under its pressure, the metamorphosis of the human form is downward, toward the worms of Beckett, the insect people and sentient ooze of Burroughs.[21]

Like Harari, Hassan notes that such violence seems inexpressible: "Literature, turning against itself, aspires to silence" (3). Relying on "radical irony" (9), "literature strives for silence by accepting chance and improvisation; its principle becomes indeterminacy" (10). All

---

[21] Ihab Hassan, "The Literature of Silence," in *The Postmodern Turn: Essays in Postmodern Theory and Culture* (Columbus: Ohio State University Press, 1987), 4.

these features of postmodernism were present throughout the last century.

The aspiration to silence that Hassan perceives in mid-century writing is also explained as trauma. Trauma theory, despite disagreements among its proponents, has become the primary way to account for the difficulty of speaking about violence. Like Taylor and Harari, some trauma theorists speak of secularity and the sublime. For example, Dominick LaCapra characterizes secularity itself as a trauma: "The hiddenness, death, or absence of a radically transcendent divinity or of absolute foundations makes of existence a fundamentally traumatic scene in which anxiety threatens to color and perhaps confuse, all relations."[22] He associates this crisis with the sublime:

> Moreover, on a somewhat different level, there has been an important tendency in modern culture and thought to convert trauma into the occasion for sublimity, to transvalue it into a test of the self or the group and an entry into the extraordinary. In the sublime, the excess of trauma becomes an uncanny source of elation or ecstasy.... They [violent events] may also give rise to what may be termed founding traumas—traumas that paradoxically become the valorized or intensely cathected basis of identity for an individual or a group rather than events that pose the problematic question of identity. (164–65)

This view of trauma as a foundation of collective and personal identity depends on communal knowledge of historical events.

---

[22] Dominick LaCapra, "Writing History, Writing Trauma," in *Writing and Revising the Disciplines*, ed. Jonathan Monroe (Ithaca, NY: Cornell University Press, 2002), 165.

In contrast, in *Unclaimed Experience: Trauma, Narrative, and History*, Cathy Caruth defines trauma as a specific event that is not known: "trauma is not locatable in the simple violent or original event in an individual's past, but rather in the way that its very unassimilated nature—the way it was precisely *not known* in the first instance—returns to haunt the survivor later on."[23] The victim becomes aware of trauma by its effects: "The historical power of the trauma is not just that the experience is repeated after its forgetting, but that it is only in and through its inherent forgetting that it is first experienced at all" (17). Perhaps "not registering" the experience would be more accurate than "forgetting." Caruth speaks of trauma as both the violent event and the psychic injury.[24] Like a physical blow that makes a person black out, trauma is a complete break in consciousness.

Since the victim is incapable of remembering the traumatic experience, others are needed to reconstruct it. In an interview with Caruth, Dori Laub, a psychoanalyst who works with Holocaust survivors, assigns this task to historians, therapists, and writers:

> You know, a historian is more attentive to the facts and to the written document, or even the written testimony by the Germans—which is valid, though it is not survivors' testimony. The psychoanalyst is more attentive to the internal reality and has a difficult time with the external reality. With the literary scholar, it's imagination. It's

---

[23] Cathy Caruth, *Unclaimed Experience: Trauma, Narrative, and History* (Baltimore: Johns Hopkins University Press, 1996), 4.

[24] Caruth traces the development of Freud's concept of trauma from *Beyond the Pleasure Principle* to *Moses and Monotheism* in Chapter 3 of *Unclaimed Experience*.

not limited to reality. It continues a back-and-forth flow between reality and imagination.[25]

This concept of trauma informs Laub's position on the ethical issue of bearing witness to violence. He claims: "The historical imperative to bear witness could essentially *not be met during the actual occurrence.*"[26] Providing an example of the writer bearing witness for the victim, Shoshana Felman cites Albert Camus's *The Plague*:

The specific task of the literary testimony is, in other words, to open up in that belated witness, which the reader now historically becomes, the imaginative capability of perceiving history—what is happening to others—*in one's own body*, with the power of sight (of insight) usually afforded only by one's own immediate physical involvement.

It is thus that the literary testimony of *The Plague* offers its *historical eyewitnessing in the flesh.*[27]

Although Felman's italicized phrase echoes Harari's term "flesh-witnessing," her concept is not at all the same. Where Harari argues that victims possess the knowledge to testify, Felman and Laub transfer the responsibility for bearing witness to experts, particularly writers:

[25] Cathy Caruth, *Listening to Trauma: Conversations with Leaders in the Theory and Treatment of Catastrophic Experience* (Baltimore: Johns Hopkins University Press, 2014), 58.

[26] Dori Laub, M.D., "An Event without a Witness: Truth, Testimony and Survival," in *Testimony: Crises of Witnessing in Literature, Psychoanalysis, and History*, ed. Shoshana Felman and Dori Laub, M.D. (New York: Routledge, 1992), 84.

[27] Shoshana Felman, "Camus' *The Plague*, or a Monument to Witnessing," in *Testimony: Crises of Witnessing in Literature, Psychoanalysis, and History*, ed. Shoshana Felman and Dori Laub, M.D. (New York: Routledge, 1992), 108–9.

[*Testimony*] is then a book about how art inscribes (artistically bears witness to) *what we do not yet know of our lived historical relation to events of our times.*

In considering, in this way, literature and art as a precocious mode of witnessing—of accessing reality—when all other modes of knowledge are precluded, our ultimate concern has been with the preservation, in this book, both of the uniqueness of experience in the face of its theorization, and of the shock of the unintelligible in the face of the attempt at its interpretation.[28]

The writer becomes the witness, because the victim is incapable of giving testimony.

The displacement of witnessing from the victim to other people divides trauma theorists. Disagreeing with Caruth, Felman, and Laub, Ruth Leys criticizes the "powerful trend in the humanities to recognize in the experience of trauma, especially the trauma of the Holocaust, a fundamental crisis for historical representation (and at the limit, for representation as such)."[29] She objects to the view that violence is inexpressible, because it "leads to doubts about the veracity of the victim's testimony: to the extent that the traumatic occurrence is considered never to have become part of the victim's ordinary memory, it is unclear how she can truthfully testify" about a violent event (298). Supporting Leys's critique, Susannah Radstone argues that Caruth's model is untrue to psychoanalytic principles. The idea that the "act of 'recovery' takes place in relation

[28] Shoshana Felman and Dori Laub, M.D., "Foreword," in *Testimony: Crises of Witnessing in Literature, Psychoanalysis, and History,* ed. Shoshana Felman and Dori Laub, M.D. (New York: Routledge, 1992), xx.

[29] Ruth Leys, *Trauma: A Genealogy* (Chicago: University of Chicago Press, 2000), 16.

to a *witness*," she points out, invests the analyst "with immensely and conclusively authoritative interpretive capacities."[30] She objects that Caruth "dispenses with the layering of the conscious/subconscious and unconscious, substituting for them a conscious mind in which past experiences are accessible, and a dissociated area of the mind from which traumatic past experiences cannot be accessed" (16). Radstone, in contrast, wants to restore Freud's emphasis on the "unconscious production of associations to a memory, rather than qualities intrinsic to certain events, that is understood to render a memory traumatic" (16). For Radstone, trauma is not a collective experience but an individual reaction to violence: "it is not an event, which is by its nature 'toxic' to the mind, but what the mind later does to memory" (17). Accordingly, "the traumatization effect does not appear to reside in the nature of the event. Some need no support after a so-called trauma, while others need help" (17). This distinction preserves the medical meaning of trauma as a diagnosis for individual victims while acknowledging that other responses to violence are possible.

Rooted in psychoanalysis, trauma theory seeks ways to heal victims of violence when their inability to describe their injury perpetuates painful symptoms. But this model does not fit everyone who experiences violence. Harari provides extensive evidence of a different reaction to extreme experience. Whereas Caruth and other trauma theorists posit a hole in consciousness, Harari shows that

---

[30] Susannah Radstone, "Trauma Theory: Contexts, Politics, Ethics," *Paragraph* 30 (2007): 20, 24. Radstone is wary of specific reconstructions proposed by analysts or writers that ignore the recent "opening up of texts to multiple, contestable, divergent or contradictory readings" and "the situated, local and multiple readings of historically specific readers and audiences" (24).

many soldiers feel they have gained sublime insights. Where trauma theory attributes the inexpressibility of violence to a deficiency in the victim, Harari argues that violence is inexpressible because only those who have experienced it can understand it. The deficiency is in the audience, not the initiate.

Soldiers were not the only ones who confronted violence, and Harari's observations apply to civilians as well. The conviction that extreme experience reveals truths that are incommunicable permeates twentieth-century writing. In *Heart of Darkness*, Marlow says to his companions, "You can't understand? How could you— with solid pavement under your feet" (49), a question that many twentieth-century writers reiterate. When they speak of the difficulty of describing events, they too imply that the problem is not their lack of knowledge but the reader's lack of experience. Like the soldiers Harari studies, twentieth-century writers continually say they are unable to describe horrific events but do not stop trying. They feel responsible for representing the violence of their times even though they question the possibility of succeeding.

Despite the political divisions of the century, writers faced the same rhetorical dilemma and learned from one another. The authors I discuss found models across national and period boundaries. English and German texts influenced each other, and postcolonial authors followed European examples. These writers not only felt the urgency of representing the nightmares of their time but also wrestled with similar ethical and aesthetic questions: If only victims have authoritative knowledge of violence, how can a writer convey their experience? If the testimony of victims is not forthcoming or accurate or convincing, can a writer speak for them? Does a writer's lack of authentic experience invalidate an imagined narrative? Do the vicarious emotions produced by the work of art desecrate victims' suffering? Does aesthetic form diminish or intensify the gravity of violence? Are realistic accounts of events more ethical than symbolic representations? Writers addressed these questions explicitly in their essays, memoirs, and letters and implicitly in their literary texts. Taylor and Harari show how secularity and Sensationism framed these questions.

The "fragilization" of beliefs made authors suspicious of positivist claims. To describe violent events without imposing a meaning on them, the writers I consider developed a set of strategies that make the meaning of their narratives indeterminate. Finding that neither realism nor symbolism could convey the nightmares of contemporary violence, they attached symbolic meanings to actual events. Extremity, excess, and irony push readers beyond the empirical referent toward multiple symbolic meanings. Extreme form and content are transgressive and volatile. Excessive detail in plot, character, and description sustains innumerable patterns. Irony keeps the meaning of statements uncertain. In addition, parallels between similar events, each described realistically, preserve their specificity. Using these strategies, writers were able to represent contemporary events without assigning a particular meaning to them. Indeterminate texts may not have legal weight or bear witness to specific acts, but they allowed authors in a secular culture to respond to violence.[31]

---

[31] See also Michael Rothberg, *Traumatic Realism: The Demands of Holocaust Representation* (Minneapolis and London: University of Minnesota Press, 2000), 9: "There can be no assumption, of course, of a direct access to history. The critique of representation ... has aroused an unavoidable suspicion about naïve claims of realism," and "In the representation of a historical event, in other words, a text's 'realist' component seeks strategies for referring to and documenting the world; its 'modernist' side questions its ability to document history transparently; and its 'postmodern' moment responds to the economic and political conditions of its emergence and public circulation."

Although the problem of representing unimaginable violence persisted, confidence in the possibility of expressing inner experience diminished as the years passed. My examples mark points on this downward slope. I chose writers who addressed the rhetorical dilemma of the period and acknowledged the influence of their predecessors. Other writers, male and female, faced this dilemma as well, but the canonical figures I discuss became models. In the early years of the century, Symbolists and Expressionists tried to create nonreligious versions of spiritual experience by turning away from the visible world. After the First World War, however, writers and artists distrusted the ambiguity of abstraction, and they tried to ground nonempirical experience in empirical reality. Post-Expressionist paintings and modernist and magic realist texts illustrate the duality of realism and symbolism in the interwar period. After the Second World War, this duality of thing and meaning broke down. Postmodern writers became skeptical of representation itself, and some writers turned back to the material world that Symbolists had scorned. In *The Tin Drum*, Günter Grass portrays ordinary objects as better witnesses than people, and in *Austerlitz* W. G. Sebald grants agency to things. Matter came to seem more trustworthy than memory.

These rhetorical claims anticipate the ontological assumptions of thing theory and other new materialisms. Rita Felski describes the "radical empiricism" of such approaches, including "animal studies, thing theory, ecological thought, the posthuman—all fields premised on the intertwinement and codependence of human and nonhuman actors."[32] Such "leveling of phenomena through their incorporation

---

[32] Rita Felski, "Latour and Literary Studies," *PMLA* 130 (2015): 737–38.

into networks" (738), she notes, "steers us away from monocausal explanations of what and how a text signifies" (739). The new materialists' distrust of any single narrative extends Taylor's analysis of secularity to the present. Where he calls attention to multiple beliefs, however, new materialisms focus on the interaction of many agents. No longer turning to symbolism for immaterial meaning, late-century writers find meaning in things.

I begin with the Symbolist response to the late nineteenth-century crisis of belief. In 1880, Matthew Arnold had predicted that poetry would perform the services of religion and philosophy: "More and more mankind will discover that we have to turn to poetry to interpret life for us, to console us, to sustain us. Without poetry, our science will appear incomplete; and most of what now passes with us for religion and philosophy will be replaced by poetry."[33] By the turn of the century Arthur Symons was able to identify a group of poets who accomplished this feat. Symons's *The Symbolist Movement in Literature* appeared in 1899, the same year that Joseph Conrad published *Heart of Darkness*. Conrad's narrative discusses and dramatizes the instability of meaning in a secular world, and Chapter 1 shows how *Heart of Darkness* embeds Conrad's eyewitness knowledge of colonial brutality in layers of symbolic meaning. He was first praised and then excoriated for this solution to the problem of representing the horror of colonialism. In 1975, Chinua Achebe charged that *Heart of Darkness* was a racist text, and since then critics have debated his objection to the work. In my view, much of the case against Conrad is a case against symbolism.

---

[33] Matthew Arnold, "The Study of Poetry," in *Complete Prose Works of Matthew Arnold, Vol. 9: English Literature and Irish Politics*, ed. R. H. Super (Ann Arbor: University of Michigan, 1973), 161–62.

At the turn of the century, colonial abuses seemed far from Europe, but the effects of secularity that Taylor observes are evident in the tormented art of the period. In contrast to Symbolists' aim of replacing the discourses of religion and philosophy, Expressionists focused on emotion. They experimented with distortion and abstraction to represent inner experience rather than material reality. Much of their work conveys personal pain, but the personal also represents a general longing for meaning. Secularity contributed to the anxiety and uncertainty that was generalized as angst. In retrospect, this angst may seem unwarranted, but it influenced initial responses to the First World War.

Although the Expressionist representation of intense feeling was a welcome alternative to the reigning materialism of bourgeois society, it later stirred up enthusiasm for the First World War. As Milton A. Cohen writes of the Expressionist generation, "One could almost say the prewar modernists *embodied* war …. For their relationship with war was essentially symbolic and symbiotic: as they drew energy from the *idea* of war, their own energies, in turn, were quickly sucked into the real war's immeasurably larger vortex."[34] Thomas Mann ruefully recalled the prewar mood: "War! We felt its coming as a purification, a liberation, and an immense hope. This is what the poets spoke of, only of this."[35] War metaphorically provided the intensity Expressionists cultivated. When the metaphor became reality, however, there was a reaction against all aspects of prewar life, including Expressionist art. Its abstract forms seemed

[34] Milton A. Cohen, "Fatal Symbiosis: Modernism and World War I," *War, Literature and the Arts* 8 (1996): 2.
[35] Quoted in Cohen, "Fatal Symbiosis," 25.

too ambiguous and too malleable, and its embrace of violent change seemed perverse. Actual violence is more spectacular than emotional turmoil, but both kinds of pain seemed inexpressible. As Harari shows, when feelings are the foundation of truth, the objective gravity of the situation is not what victims record. Attempts to portray extreme emotion continued from prewar Expressionism to postwar art, though the violence of inner experience was dwarfed by the actual destruction of war. The postwar reaction recalibrated the balance of realism and symbolism, grounding meaning in a particular time and place.

Expressionism emerged in Central Europe, but it also influenced English writing. T. S. Eliot and D. H. Lawrence were familiar with avant-garde German art before 1914, and they absorbed the aims and methods of Expressionism. Having been part of the prewar movement, Eliot and Lawrence also participated in the postwar reaction. Like many others, they tried to ground meaning in recognizable material reality. Chapter 2 examines the transition from Expressionism to Post-Expressionism in Eliot, and Chapter 3 traces the same development in Lawrence. The differences between Eliot's "The Love Song of J. Alfred Prufrock" and *The Waste Land* and between Lawrence's *The Rainbow* and *Women in Love* illustrate the contrast between Expressionist ambiguity and modernist indeterminacy.

Joyce wrote *Ulysses* in Zurich during the war, though it deflects the recent political violence in Ireland to a day in Dublin in 1904. Like Lawrence, Joyce avoids direct references to the war, but responds to it with a radically indeterminate mixture of extreme realism and extreme symbolism. Eliot recognized the historical immediacy of the book, and he praised *Ulysses* as a breakthrough in making the modern

world possible for art. He called attention to Joyce's disruption of
the narrative conventions of realism and symbolism and his use of
parallels between past and present. In Germany, the art historian Franz
Roh perceived a similar strategy in Continental painting and literature.
Emphasizing the difference between prewar and postwar art, Roh
called the new movement "Post-Expressionism" and "Magic Realism."
He theorized it as a tension between object and spirit. This movement
was also known as "New Objectivity," a name that emphasizes its
focus on material reality rather than its duality. Chapter 4 argues that
the features of *Ulysses* that Eliot identified resemble the characteristics
of postwar German art that Roh described.

Just as European Expressionism influenced Eliot and Lawrence,
the impact of *Ulysses* reached German writers, including Alfred
Döblin and Günter Grass, as well as postcolonial writers, including
Gabriel García Márquez and Salman Rushdie. Döblin's *Berlin
Alexanderplatz* stands at the intersection of English and German
responses to the war, and Chapter 5 follows the route from *Ulysses*
and *Berlin Alexanderplatz* to late-century magic realism. Döblin
provided a model for Günter Grass's *The Tin Drum*, as Grass, in turn,
provided a model for Salman Rushdie's *Midnight's Children*. García
Márquez also acknowledged the importance of *Ulysses* to Latin
American writers. This genealogy demonstrates that major writers
of the century turned to one another for solutions to a persistent
rhetorical problem.

Although the First World War had been called a "holocaust,"[36]
the term came to describe the genocide of the Second World War.

---

[36] Humphrey Cobb, *Paths of Glory* (New York: Penguin, 2010), 65.

The field of Holocaust Studies has made the Nazi death camps the locus of fierce debates about representing atrocities. W. G. Sebald entered this minefield as a German writing about Jewish victims of the Nazis, and Chapter 6 shows how he addresses the century's dilemma in *Austerlitz* (2001). Sebald suggests that things hold more meaning than any account, whether a witness's testimony or a writer's story. In contrast to the ironic and symbolic animation of objects in magic realism, Sebald is dead earnest about the meaning of things. Going further than Grass, he grants agency to things and constructs characters and narratives as if they were machines with interchangeable parts.

Sebald criticized Grass for failing to portray Jews' experience of the Second World War, and in *Austerlitz* he turns to H. G. Adler for a victim's testimony. Adler wrote a documentary account of the Theresienstadt camp, but he was an artist as well as a survivor. His trilogy about the period begins with *Panorama*, a novel deeply influenced by Joyce's *A Portrait of the Artist as a Young Man*. *Panorama* discusses and demonstrates how symbolic forms can and cannot represent historical events. In *The Wall*, the final novel in his trilogy, Adler takes Harari's logic to the limit. The narrator disqualifies survivors as witnesses, telling an acquaintance, "I don't know if I was all that directly involved. I didn't in fact die, and therefore I don't know.... Only the dead were there, because they alone remained. The rest of us only passed through."[37] This conjunction of Grass, Sebald, and Adler is the culmination of themes I trace in other writers. The twentieth-century quest

---

[37] H. G. Adler, *The Wall*, trans. Peter Filkins (New York: Random House, 2014), 186.

for immaterial meaning that began with Symbolism ended. For Sebald, no narrative is as reliable as material objects. Things are the repository of meaning. They are meaningful as physical evidence, not as symbols.

The secular century ended in the United States on September 11, 2001, not because the attacks on the World Trade Center were carried out by religious terrorists but because the immediate—and short-lived—aftermath was national unity. The attacks made people long for a communal response, and indeterminacy was unacceptable for a time. Writers again turned to the examples of the past, but they replaced the irony of the twentieth century with solemnity. Galway Kinnell's elegy "When the Towers Fell" illustrates the new tone. The poem is indebted to *The Waste Land* but speaks for a community. This unity did not last. It broke into factions of militant believers, hunkered down, certain of their own beliefs and intolerant of others' views.

Facing the continuing need to represent horrific events in a secular period, the authors of some of the twentieth century's landmark texts adopted their predecessors' solutions. They faced different forms of violence, but variables of scale and circumstance were not their concern. They concentrated on the problem of meaning. They were all too aware that the epistemology of Sensationism and the absence of any consensus of belief made violence seem indescribable. Unwilling to impose any specific meaning on events, writers nevertheless accepted the responsibility of responding to public crises. While Taylor and Harari account for the difficulty of writing about violence in a secular age, my aim is to show how some of the great writers of the period expressed the inexpressible.

1

Symbolism in a secular age

Heart of Darkness appeared the same year that Arthur Symons published *The Symbolist Movement in Literature*, and both texts respond to the period's secularity. Symons takes the demise of faith for granted and embraces the Symbolist Movement as a turn-of-the-century aesthetic substitute. He interprets the movement as a fight "against exteriority, against rhetoric, against a materialistic tradition," and he praises Symbolist poets for seeking the kind of meaning that religious faith provides.[1] The "conscious" construction of symbols (3), Symons explains, performs a spiritual function: "in speaking to us so intimately, so solemnly, as only religion had hitherto spoken to us, [literature] becomes itself a kind of religion, with all the duties and responsibilities of the sacred ritual" (9). Like other writers of the time, Joseph Conrad reacted to the loss of unifying religious beliefs by searching for alternative versions of nonempirical experience. Conrad did not make his art a substitute for religion, but he did turn to symbolism to resist economic and philosophical materialism. His use of symbolism in *Heart of Darkness* to represent the violence of

---

[1] Arthur Symons, *The Symbolist Movement in Literature* (London: Constable, 1908), 8–9.

colonialism became a prototype for later responses to the nightmares of history. The use of symbolism also became the target of scathing ethical and political attacks, notably by Chinua Achebe and Fredric Jameson.

Using Roman Jakobson's structural definition of symbolism, we can begin to understand why Conrad and so many other twentieth-century writers found symbolism useful, as well as the reasons that so many critics have objected to it. Jakobson graphs language on a horizontal axis of syntax and a vertical axis of semantics.[2] He compares syntax to the figure of metonymy because both are based on contiguity, and he associates semantics with metaphor because both depend on substitution in a given position (78). Extending this model to literary forms, Jakobson argues that realism, which refers to observable reality, is metonymic, and symbolism, which can evoke referents beyond sensory experience, is metaphoric.[3] Just as every sentence operates on both the syntactic axis and the semantic axis, every text has realistic and symbolic significance.

Jakobson's linguistic model clarifies the relation between realism and symbolism in *Heart of Darkness*. The specificity of realism represents historical conditions, and the multiple meanings of symbolism frustrate attempts to explain events. Conrad signals symbolic meaning by embedding realistic events in various discourses. For example, as Marlow steams upstream, he speaks with the precision of an official report: "It was just two months from the day we left the creek when

[2] Roman Jakobson and Morris Halle, *Fundamentals of Language* (The Hague: Mouton de Gruyter, 1956), 60.
[3] See also David Lodge, *The Modes of Modern Writing* (Ithaca, NY: Cornell University Press, 1977). Lodge extends Jakobson's remarks in a detailed comparison of realism and symbolism.

we came to the bank below Kurtz's station."[4] These coordinates of time and place are empirical details that establish the verisimilitude of realism. In the next sentence, however, Marlow posits a completely different kind of meaning: "Going up that river was like travelling back to the earliest beginnings of the world, when vegetation rioted on the earth and the big trees were kings" (33). The animistic metaphors suggest an imagined world that is primordial, prehistoric, primitive, and mythic. This oscillation between the empirical referent and nonempirical associations connects historical events to multiple patterns of symbolic meaning.

References to a particular time and place are the end point of realism but the starting point of symbolism. Conrad needed both forms to represent the nightmare of colonialism. He had witnessed the brutality of colonialism in the Belgian Congo, but instead of writing a strictly realistic account of his personal experience, he added multiple symbolic patterns to his story. As the frame narrator says, Marlow is a "seaman" for whom "the meaning of an episode was not inside like a kernel but outside, enveloping the tale which brought it out only as a glow brings out a haze" (5). The multiple meanings of symbolism in a secular period produce such a haze, and Marlow makes the difficulty of describing and understanding his African journey part of his tale.

Conrad's diverse explanations of the European presence in Africa illustrate the absence of consensus that Charles Taylor associates with secularity. As Taylor explains, when there is a loss of "publicly available orders of meaning," the proliferation of beliefs weakens the

---

[4] Conrad, *Heart of Darkness*, 33.

authority of each one.[5] Marlow says that his reason for going to Africa is that as a child he was captivated by the continent. It was one of the "blank spaces on the earth," though by the time he arrived "it was not a blank space any more."[6] His anecdote conveys a boy's naïve wish for an adventure that would leave a mark on the world. Others have different motives. The Belgian Company's doctor confides that he has a scientific interest in Africa: "I have a little theory which you Messieurs who go out there must help me to prove. This is my share in the advantages my country shall reap from the possession of such a magnificent dependency" (12). Marlow's aunt speaks of "weaning those ignorant millions from their horrid ways," though Marlow considers her view of colonialism "humbug," and he ventures "to hint that the Company was run for profit" (12). The Eldorado Exploring Expedition comes to Africa for its riches. Although the name of the group echoes Marlow's boyhood wish, these Europeans are nothing more than "sordid buccaneers," no better than "burglars breaking into a safe" (30). A variety of reasons for being in Africa—adventure, knowledge, westernization, fortune—drives the colonial enterprise.

But individual motives are inadequate when they lead to violence. Witnessing the casual and opportunistic cruelty of colonialism, Marlow claims that a transcendent belief, an idea, is necessary to justify it:

> The conquest of the earth, which mostly means the taking it away from those who have a different complexion or slightly flatter noses than ourselves, is not a pretty thing when you look into it

---

[5] Taylor, A Secular Age, 353.
[6] Conrad, Heart of Darkness, 8.

too much. What redeems it is the idea only. An idea at the back of it, not a sentimental pretence but an idea; and an unselfish belief in the idea—something you can set up, and bow down before, and offer a sacrifice to. (7)

Religion no longer sustains this kind of belief, and Marlow's longing for a redeeming idea seems sincere. The narrative, however, undermines his ethical justification of conquest by introducing Kurtz, who becomes a node of symbolic meanings. As Marlow says, "All Europe contributed to the making of Kurtz" (49). Kurtz expounds the big ideas circulating in Europe at the time. He is reputed to be a journalist, a politician of indeterminate convictions, a scientist, a painter, and a musician. He speaks of love to the young Russian and promises profits to the Company. Kurtz has too many attributes and too many professions. This excess undermines the credibility of each one. By the time Marlow describes him as a "universal genius" (72), the words ironically suggest something more like a con man. The succession of identities that Kurtz assumes is an individual manifestation of the surplus of beliefs Taylor observes in a secular culture. Instead of committing himself to any of these beliefs, Kurtz installs himself as an object of worship: "unspeakable rites" are "offered up to him" (50). Marlow's justification of conquest and Kurtz's transgression are both expressed as forms of worship. The parallel between setting up an idea and setting up oneself as something to "bow down before" demonstrates how easy it is to conflate grand ideas and selfish desires.

   In his encounter with Kurtz, Marlow confronts the consequences of actions based on merely personal beliefs: "I had to deal with a being to whom I could not appeal in the name of anything high or low. I had, even like the niggers, to invoke him—himself—his own exalted and incredible degradation" (66). The two men have no shared beliefs to ground the meaning of their words. Their impasse is not uncommon, and Marlow calls attention to other examples of the malleability of language. In the colonial vocabulary, natives are "enemies" (14), and indentured African laborers are "criminals" (16). On being told that Kurtz's victims were rebels, Marlow exclaims, "Rebels! What would be the next definition I was to hear. There had been enemies, criminals, workers—and these were— rebels" (58). This instability of meaning gives his conversations with Kurtz "the terrific suggestiveness of words heard in dreams, of phrases spoken in nightmares" (66). Just as realism fails to express nightmares, it is incapable of conveying Marlow's extreme experience. Like his contemporaries and successors, Conrad turned to symbolism.

The most provocative source of symbolism in the text is extremity, particularly transgressive extremity. As Michel Foucault argues, the impact of transgression is inherently symbolic.[7] Realistic descriptions of extremity convey the particularity of an event—what happened— and symbolic associations convey its impact—how it felt. Marlow uses both strategies to express his astonishment when he sees Kurtz's house:

---

[7] Michel Foucault, *The History of Sexuality*, vol. 1, trans. Robert Hurley (New York: Pantheon, 1978), 7. Foucault's example of extremity is breaking taboos about sexual discourse. He claims that any transgression produces meanings beyond those of the act itself: "Something that smacks of revolt, of promised freedom, of the coming age of a different law, slips easily into this discourse on sexual oppression. Some of the ancient functions of prophecy are reactivated therein."

These round knobs were not ornamental but symbolic; they were expressive and puzzling, striking and disturbing—food for thought and also for vultures if there had been any looking down from the sky; but at all events for such ants as were industrious enough to ascend the pole. They would have been even more impressive, those heads on the stakes, if their faces had not been turned to the house.[8]

This passage shows how objects become symbols. Marlow's reaction begins in empirical description, but the shock of realizing that he is looking at human skulls transforms them from the "ornamental" to the "symbolic." The extremity of the objects causes them to accumulate additional meanings that are both empirical and nonempirical. The "knobs" become "expressive," "puzzling," "striking," "disturbing"—they are "food for thought," as well as for vultures and ants. This multiplicity, the capacity of the empirical referent to be itself and something else, represents violence without explaining it.

When *Heart of Darkness* appeared in *Blackwood's Magazine* in 1899, the proliferation of symbolic meanings fed the hunger for nonreligious sources of meaning. In *Conrad in the Nineteenth Century*, Ian Watt argues that *Heart of Darkness* "belongs to a specifically symbolic tradition of fiction, and it is the only one of Conrad's novels which does."[9] Like Taylor, Watt associates symbolism with the breakdown of religious belief. He argues that "Marlow is confronting a general intellectual and moral impasse...and this

[8] Conrad, *Heart of Darkness*, 57.
[9] Ian Watt, *Conrad in the Nineteenth Century* (Berkeley and Los Angeles: University of California Press, 1979), 188.

gap, in turn, can be seen in a wider historical and philosophical perspective as a reflection of the same breakdown of the shared categories of understanding and judgment, as had originally imposed on Conrad and many of his contemporaries the indirect, subjective, and guarded strategies that characterized the expressive modes of Symbolism" (195). Conrad dramatizes this breakdown in Marlow's reaction to Kurtz. Close to death, in a state of "extremity," Kurtz whispers, "The horror! The horror!"[10] Like someone who encounters the sublime, Kurtz is incapable of saying more. This is the "supreme moment of complete knowledge" (69), yet it is inexpressible. Marlow ponders these words at length. By the time he visits Kurtz's Intended, the possible meanings even include her name. He tells her: "The last word he pronounced was—your name" (77).

The ambiguity of Kurtz's last words troubles critics. Patrick Brantlinger, for example, cites the diversity of interpretations of Kurtz's utterance as evidence that the symbolism in the text cancels "external referents."[11] He argues, "Conrad overlays the political and moral content of his novella with symbolic and mythic patterns that divert attention from Kurtz and the Congo to misty halos and moonshine" (387). Brantlinger assumes that symbolic and mythic patterns undermine political and moral meanings. He prefers the specific "external referents" of realism because they connect meaning to a particular time and place.

In contrast to Brantlinger's uneasiness with multiple meanings, Marlow accepts uncertainty. He interprets Kurtz's cry symbolically,

---

[10] Conrad, *Heart of Darkness*, 69–70.
[11] Patrick Brantlinger, "Imperialism, Impressionism, and the Politics of Style," in *Heart of Darkness*, 4th edn., ed. Paul B. Armstrong (New York: Norton, 2006), 389.

that is, as the foundation of a structure that allows innumerable possibilities: "I saw on that ivory face the expression of sombre pride, of ruthless power, of craven terror—of an intense and hopeless despair."[12] Whatever Kurtz means by "The horror!" the word constitutes a judgment. The judgment itself is less important than Kurtz's willingness to judge. In the absence of moral principles, "He had summed up—he had judged. 'The horror!' He was a remarkable man" (70). In a secular period, this passes as an achievement: "After all, this was the expression of some sort of belief; it had candour, it had conviction, it had a vibrating note of revolt in its whisper, it had the appalling face of a glimpsed truth—the strange commingling of desire and hate" (70). Although Kurtz's last words do not affirm a specific meaning, Marlow regards them as a revelation. Kurtz's truth, like the sublime, is inexpressible and incontrovertible.

Watt regards this indeterminacy as a weakness in the narrative. He recognizes that symbolism changed in response to the "the intellectual crisis of the late nineteenth century, a crisis by now most familiar to literary history in its twin manifestations of the death of God and the disappearance of the omniscient author."[13] Like Taylor, Watt notes that the relation between particular objects or events and "some larger, nonliteral meaning" was not controversial when "everything in the outside world was widely agreed to constitute a fixed order, in which each item had its appropriate religious, moral or social role" (181). Once this order disappeared, personal meanings made symbolism indeterminate, and Watt questions the value of this change: "There is some doubt, however, whether

---

[12] Conrad, *Heart of Darkness*, 69.
[13] Watt, *Conrad in the Nineteenth Century*, 181.

either impressionism or symbolism stand for meanings which are sufficiently clear to be worth using" (181). This doubt is the negative side of symbolic indeterminacy, and it is the basis of many objections to *Heart of Darkness*.

Perhaps the most influential objection is Chinua Achebe's incendiary charge that *Heart of Darkness* is a racist text. His argument is based on Conrad's mixture of symbolism and historical realism. Achebe cites specific passages that are clearly racist, but he does not rely on this evidence, because it "might be contended, of course, that the attitude to the African in *Heart of Darkness* is not Conrad's but that of his fictional narrator, Marlow, and that far from endorsing it Conrad might indeed be holding it up to irony and criticism."[14] Instead, Achebe targets the symbolic elements of a text that refers to actual events, people, and places. He attacks the rhetoric that signals symbolic meanings by repeating F. R. Leavis's mockery of Conrad's "adjectival insistence upon inexpressible and incomprehensible mystery" in sentences such as, "*It was the stillness of an implacable force brooding over an inscrutable intention*" (338). Achebe considers this kind of discourse irresponsible:

> When a writer while pretending to record scenes, incidents and their impact is in reality engaged in inducing hypnotic stupor in his readers through a bombardment of emotive words and other forms of trickery much more has to be at stake than stylistic felicity. (338)

Distrusting a style that reaches for more than empirical experience, Achebe advocates realism. Three quarters of a century into the secular

---

[14] Chinua Achebe, "An Image of Africa: Racism in Conrad's *Heart of Darkness*," in *Heart of Darkness*, 4th edn., ed. Paul B. Armstrong (New York: Norton, 2006), 342.

age, the multiple meanings of symbolism seem a form of "trickery." Achebe reverses Arthur Symons's assessment of visible and invisible realities and indicts Conrad for writing about Africa symbolically:

> Africa as setting and backdrop which eliminates the African as human factor. Africa as a metaphysical battlefield devoid of all recognizable humanity, into which the wandering European enters at his peril. Can nobody see the preposterous and perverse arrogance in thus reducing Africa to the role of props for the break-up of one petty European mind? (343–44)

Using Africa as a "metaphysical battlefield," Conrad dehumanizes and "depersonalizes" Africans (344).

Conrad, however, was more interested in actual violence than the "metaphysical" kind. Africa is not "setting and backdrop" for "the break-up of one petty European mind"; Africa is Conrad's subject. Europeans are the "human factor" in the text because they are responsible for the violence. Conrad intended *Heart of Darkness* to protest Belgian atrocities. In 1898, he wrote his publisher:

> The criminality of inefficiency and pure selfishness when tackling the civilizing work in Africa is a justifiable idea. The subject is of our time distinc[t]ly—though not topically treated. It is a story as much as my *Outpost of Progress* was but, so to speak "takes in" more—is a little wider—is less concentrated upon individuals.[15]

In rhetorical terms, Achebe regards European anxiety as the tenor of the metaphor and myths about Africa as its vehicle. In contrast,

---

[15] Joseph Conrad, *Collected Letters of Joseph Conrad*, vol. 2, ed. Frederick R. Karl and Laurence Davies (Cambridge: Cambridge University Press, 1986), 139–40.

I am arguing that Conrad regards events in Africa as the tenor, and the allusions to myth, psychology, politics, and art are its vehicles. The violence in the text is not a symbol of a European crisis but a brutal historical fact that Conrad represents through a combination of empirical description and symbolic patterns. The abuse of Africans was all too obvious to him, if not to all Europeans, so he focuses on the perpetrators, asking a question that recurred throughout the century: how could "civilized" people do such things?

Marlow's first words begin to answer this question. He undermines the assumption that Europe is inherently superior to Africa by drawing a parallel between Africa and England: "'And this also,' said Marlow suddenly, 'has been one of the dark places of the earth.'"[16] He adds, "I was thinking of very old times, when the Romans first came here, nineteen hundred years ago" (5). To make sense of his extraordinary experiences, he aligns the European presence in Africa with the Roman occupation of Britain: "But darkness was here yesterday" (6). He spells out the correspondence: the "savagery," the "wilderness," and the "hearts of wild men" were "here" (6). Unlike a comparison, his parallel preserves the distinctiveness of each time and place yet forms a pattern. This structure is an example of the mythical method that T. S. Eliot identified in *Ulysses*, and it reappears throughout the century.

The alternative Achebe proposes reveals the full extent of his indictment. He wants Africans to be portrayed realistically as complex individuals whose existence is independent of their meaning for Western readers. Achebe compares Conrad to Marco Polo, chastising

---

[16] Conrad, *Heart of Darkness*, 5.

both for representing a historical population from the perspective of an outsider: "Indeed travellers can be blind."[17] The West should "look at Africa not through a haze of distortions and cheap mystifications but quite simply as a continent of people—not angels, but not rudimentary souls either—just people" (348). Advocating realistic narratives, Achebe sacrifices too much. Symbolism is a way out of the rhetorical dilemma that secularity presents.

The consequences of adhering to Achebe's strictures are evident in Fredric Jameson's long-standing opposition to modernist symbolism. In "*Ulysses* in History" (1982), Jameson proclaims, "I believe that today, whatever our own aesthetic faults or blinkers, we have learned this particular lesson fairly well: and that for us, any art which practices symbolism is already discredited and worthless before the fact."[18] He condemns the "practice of symbolism itself, which involves the illicit transformation of existing things into so many visible or tangible meanings" (148). It seems odd to consider symbolic meanings "visible or tangible"—Symons exalts symbolism as the antithesis of the visible world. Jameson, however, implies that symbolism replaces material things with other things called meanings. Like Achebe, Jameson wants things to be just things, not a "facile affirmation that the existent also means, that things are also symbols" (148). Symbolism is a phenomenon to be studied but not valued: "Genuine interpretation ... involves the radical historisation of the form itself: what is to be interpreted is then the historical necessity for this very peculiar and complex textual structure or reading

---

[17] Achebe, "Image of Africa," 347.

[18] Fredric Jameson, "*Ulysses* in History," in *James Joyce: A Collection of Critical Essays*, ed. Mary T. Reynolds (Englewood Cliffs, NJ: Prentice-Hall, 1993), 148.

operation in the first place" (147). Symbolic form can be understood in relation to historical circumstances, but it should not be accepted as a source of meaning. His distrust of symbolism is consistent with the commitment to things in themselves articulated in thing theory and other new materialisms.

Yet when Jameson historicizes modernist symbolism, he demonstrates not its worthlessness but its value. A psychoanalytic version of symbolism guides his readings in *The Political Unconscious: Narrative as a Socially Symbolic Act* (1981). Just as Freud interprets the manifest content of the patient's statements to discover latent thoughts, Jameson probes the narrative surface to uncover ideology. Analyzing *Lord Jim*, for example, Jameson contrasts the "ostensible or manifest 'theme' of the novel" with its underlying meaning, arguing that the repeated references to honor "must mean *something else*" —his italics.[19] The search for *something else* is the essence of symbolism. In this case, the narrative theme stands for an ideological meaning. Since Jameson is operating within Marxist and Freudian systems of belief, he limits the indeterminacy that Taylor and Watt associate with a secular culture. Positing a specific symbolic meaning, Jameson argues that "modernism is itself an ideological expression of capitalism" (236) and that it "can at one and the same time be read as a Utopian compensation for everything reification brings with it" (236). His beliefs lead to a specific interpretation of the symbolic meaning of the narrative.

Jameson historicizes "Conrad's 'will to style' as a socially symbolic act" (225). Focusing on narrative point of view, Jameson approaches

---

[19] Fredric Jameson, *The Political Unconscious: Narrative as a Socially Symbolic Act* (Ithaca, NY: Cornell University Press, 1981), 217.

the epistemological question of perspective through the term "scene," because there is an "obsessive repetition" of theatrical terms such as "'scene,' 'spectacle,' and 'tableau'" in nineteenth-century fiction (231). Gustave Flaubert and Henry James, he argues, conceive of "scene" as a principle of unity: "the structural corollary of the point of view of the spectator is the unity of organization of the theatrical space and the theatrical scene" (231). In contrast, Conrad "undermines the unity of the theatrical metaphor" and "displaces" it "by transforming it into a matter of sense perception" (231–32). Whether the narrative point of view is singular or multiple, however, Jameson emphasizes that it depends on empirical observation.

The term "scene" is not only central to Jameson's symbolic reading of Conrad's style in *The Political Unconscious*, but it is also the fulcrum of his argument in "War and Representation." No longer associated with empirical perspectives, "scene" now marks the annihilation of all perspectives. Jameson introduces Kenneth Burke's "dramatistic pentad," which comprises the elements of "act, agent, agency, purpose, and scene," only to reject all elements except "scene."[20] Atrocities, Jameson explains, are "something that happens, not so much to individuals, to characters as such, as to the landscape, which fades in and out of nightmare, its mingled dialects now intelligible, now the gibberish of aliens" (1538). Invoking the trope of the indescribable nightmare, he claims that the repetition of the "same scenes of carnage and flight over and over again" is "beyond history, beyond narrative" (1538). Therefore, he argues, war cannot be represented as specific acts conducted by and to human beings.

---

[20] Fredric Jameson, "War and Representation," *PMLA* 124 (2009): 1533–34.

Only the devastation of "scene," not the experience of combatants or victims, can be described.

To illustrate the futility of attributing agency to individuals, Jameson cites two accounts of the Thirty Years' War. The first is *Der abenteuerliche Simplicissimus* (The Adventurous Simpleton) by Hans Jakob Christoffel von Grimmelshausen and dates back to 1668. The second example is *Wallenstein*, the historical novel about the Thirty Years' War that Alfred Döblin wrote during the First World War. Noting that Döblin imitates Grimmelshausen's innumerable points of view and excessive detail, Jameson comments:

> Still, we may wonder what forms the representation of agents and agency can take under the regime of the scene, in this interminable narrative of events and sequence of grotesque or nightmarish figures, more human in their caricaturality than any of the genuine human beings of realism or of our acquaintance. (1540)

"Nightmarish figures" are beyond the scope of realism. Only geographical coordinates have the stability to survive this chaos: "Scene, however, remains unnamed at this level of narrative complexity, becoming concrete in the course of the representation" (1534). Illustrating Harari's observation that violence has become indescribable, Jameson claims that the "scene" of violence can be marked but not named.

Jameson's rhetorical despair, characteristic of the twentieth century, indicates the cost of renouncing symbolism. Confronting the dilemma that earlier writers faced, he confesses to "the suspicion that war is ultimately unrepresentable" (1533). Having repudiated symbolism, Jameson upholds the ethic of incommensurability that Achebe and others promulgate. Committed to the specificity of realism, they distrust the meanings that symbolism generates. In contrast, Derek Walcott's "A Far Cry from Africa" warns that representation is inevitably tendentious. If in a secular culture the number and nature of meanings are unlimited, by multiplying the narrative patterns surrounding historical events, symbolism preserves the structure of meaning without imposing any single meaning.

Standing at the confluence of nineteenth-century realism and turn-of-the-century symbolism, *Heart of Darkness* combines these two modes to represent unimaginable violence in a secular period. Compared to the Symbolist ideal of dispensing with the visible world, *Heart of Darkness* is full of empirical detail. The symbolic patterns in the text are attached to particular referents. Notwithstanding subsequent interpretations of symbolism as an evasion of reality, Conrad achieved his political purpose. In 1909, Edmond Morel, founder of the Congo Reform Association, called *Heart of Darkness* "the most powerful thing ever written on the subject."[21] In colonial Africa, neither law nor conscience restrained well-armed Europeans far from home. As the Manager of one of the stations tells Marlow, "Anything—anything can be done in this country."[22] The unimaginable acts committed in Africa proved to be portents of the atrocities of two world wars and their aftermath. While Achebe and Jameson object to the practice of attaching symbolic meanings to realistic accounts of actual events, this strategy served a secular age by representing violence without presuming to explain it.

---

[21] Quoted in Alan Simmons, "Conrad, Casement, and the Congo Atrocities," in *Heart of Darkness*, 4th edn., ed. Paul B. Armstrong (New York: Norton, 2006), 192.

[22] Conrad, *Heart of Darkness*, 32.

2

T. S. Eliot's Expressionist angst

Colonial violence raged so far from the capitals of Europe in the first decades of the century that peace seemed stifling to avant-garde artists and writers. They were contemptuous of bourgeois complacency and eager to throw off social restraints. The Expressionist generation embraced violence as if it were a sublime truth. With the breakdown of the previous religious consensus, violence emerged as something to believe in. By 1909, the idealization of violence reached the front page of *Le Figaro* via F. T. Marinetti's Futurist manifesto. It declares: "We already live in the absolute since we have already created eternal, omnipresent speed."[1] But speed is not enough; violence is to be the absolute of the future. Violence, the manifesto claims, is the basis of art: "For art can only be violence, cruelty, and injustice" (1). War provides these qualities and more: "We want to glorify war—the world's only hygiene—militarism, patriotism, the destructive gesture of the anarchists, the beautiful ideas which kill, and contempt for woman" (1). A list of values that includes war and militarism as well as

---

[1] F. T. Marinetti, "Le Futurisme," *Le Figaro,* February 20, 1909, 1. My translation.

anarchism, beautiful ideas, and contempt for woman conveys the general need for an absolute, the more extreme the better.

Milton A. Cohen documents the extent of the rhetoric of violence in prewar art and writing. He argues that avant-garde artists spoke of war "as metaphor and as actuality, war as language, as imagery, as models of both organizing and destructive power, and most of all as focused energy."[2] Poems glorifying war appeared in the Expressionist journals *Die Aktion* and *Der Sturm.* Jakob Von Hoddis, Gottfried Benn, Georg Heym, and Georg Trakl created "images of cataclysmic war and apocalypse" (1). Although Expressionism was centered in Europe, Cohen points out that Ezra Pound voiced these themes in his poem "Sestina: Altaforte." The poem is a dramatic monologue spoken by a twelfth-century troubadour:

Damn it all! all this our South stinks peace . . . .

There's no sound like to swords swords opposing,

No cry like the battle's rejoicing

When our elbows and swords drip the crimson . . . .

Hell grant soon we hear again the swords clash!

Hell blot black for always the thought "Peace"! (1)

Pound "declaimed" these lines in a London café in 1909, the same year Marinetti published the Futurist manifesto (1).

Similarly, Alfredo Bonadeo argues that poets as different as T. E. Hulme and Rupert Brooke were convinced that war was "'the ultimate test of a nation's manhood, the ultimate proof of its vigor and of its right to exist'; it was the generation that felt that brute force is

---

[2] Cohen, "Fatal Symbiosis," 2.

manly."[3] In retrospect, it is easy to vilify these statements glorifying violence as proto-fascist propaganda, but at the time they expressed intense longing for a bedrock of meaning, whatever the particular meaning might be.[4] Although the violence in Expressionism was largely internal, prewar art and poetry prepared writers and artists to represent the unimaginable experience of the war itself.

T. S. Eliot absorbed Expressionist techniques from European writers and used them in his early poems. In 1914, Ezra Pound launched a campaign to persuade Harriet Monroe, the editor of *Poetry*, to publish Eliot's major prewar poem, "The Love Song of J. Alfred Prufrock." He told her that it had been written by the only American he knew who had "actually trained himself *and* modernized himself *on his own.*"[5] But it would be more accurate, if less superlative, to say that Eliot had been "modernized" by his contact with the European avant-garde. He wrote most of "Prufrock" in Munich during the summer of 1911, and the poem is saturated with that city's international aesthetic currents.

Although critics familiar with German literature have compared Eliot to Expressionist poets,[6] the influence of Jules Laforgue and other French Symbolists is much more widely recognized. Reviewing *Prufrock and Other Observations* for *Poetry*, Pound, for example, proclaimed that Eliot was as good as anyone writing in "French, English or American

---

[3] Alfredo Bonadeo, "War and Degradation: Gleanings from the Literature of the Great War," *Comparative Literature Studies* 21 (1984): 421.

[4] See Ho, "The Crisis of Liberalism and the Politics of Modernism," 57. Ho lists some of the monographs that link modernism and fascism.

[5] Ezra Pound, *Selected Letters of Ezra Pound, 1907–1941*, ed. D. D. Paige (New York: New Directions, 1971), 40.

[6] See Walter H. Sokel, *The Writer in Extremis: Expressionism in Twentieth-Century German Literature* (Stanford: Stanford University Press, 1959), 114.

since the death of Jules Laforgue."[7] He elaborated, "I would praise
the work for its fine tone, its humanity, and its realism; for all good
art is realism of one sort or another" (267). However, by the time Eliot
discovered Laforgue and other Symbolists in 1908, European artists and
writers had abandoned realism and lost confidence in Symbolism. In
contrast to Pound's Imagist ideal of "Direct treatment of the 'thing,'"[8] the
European avant-garde distorted things in an effort to "express" subjective
experience. Eliot became a poet during the transition from Symbolism
to Expressionism in Central Europe, and "Prufrock" is not only more
cosmopolitan than French or English, but it is more Expressionist than
realist or Symbolist. Eliot's affinities with Expressionism before the
war also illuminate the commonalities between English and German
writing in the 1920s.

In 1909, Eliot began a private notebook (published much later as
Inventions of the March Hare) just as the Expressionist movement
was coalescing. Like European painting and writing of this period,
his early poems can be read as confessions of personal anguish and
as representations of cultural angst. Jayme Stayer, for example, finds
biographical evidence of Eliot's early religious leanings, the sexual
inhibitions produced by his class and upbringing, and racism.[9] Yet
Eliot's early work—with the possible exception of the Bolo poems—
can also be read as part of the avant-garde campaign for secular
meaning, new sexual mores, and principled tolerance. While private

---

[7] Ezra Pound, Review of *Prufrock and Other Observations* by T. S. Eliot, *Poetry* 10
(August 1917): 264.
[8] Ezra Pound, "A Retrospect," in *Literary Essays of Ezra Pound*, ed. T. S. Eliot (New York:
New Directions, 1968), 3.
[9] Jayme Stayer, "Searching for the Early Eliot: *Inventions of the March Hare*," in *A Companion
to T. S. Eliot*, ed. David E. Chinitz (Oxford: Wiley-Blackwell, 2009), 112–13.

and public meanings are always present in art, Expressionists believed that the source of both kinds of meaning was subjective. Although subjectivity seems personal, their turn inward led outward. Like Expressionist art, Eliot's canonical texts of this period, "The Love Song of J. Alfred Prufrock" and "Tradition and the Individual Talent," probe private experience in search of public meaning.

Eliot had studied German since boyhood and was well prepared to enter the cultural life of Central Europe. After graduating from Harvard, he lived in Paris in the academic year 1910–1911, and he spent the summer of 1911 in Germany. His enthusiasm for German culture surprised his French friends. Replying to a letter that Eliot had sent from Munich in 1911, Alain-Fournier remarked: "I am greatly interested by what you say about the Germans. Although I was an internationalist only four or five years ago, I would now very willingly march against them. And I think the majority of Frenchmen are like me."[10] James E. Miller, Jr. speculates that Eliot joined his friend Jean Verdenal in supporting Charles Maurras and the *Action Française*,[11] but Eliot's letters suggest that he was immune to nationalist chauvinism. While on vacation in Germany in 1914, he sent Conrad Aiken an exuberant report: "I find that I like German food! I like German people! And we have five meals a day. I stuff myself; the Frau Pfarrer thinks I don't eat enough. Then I swim (there are baths) or walk (there are beautiful walks among the woods) but not far, because I must always be back in time for the next meal."[12] He

---

[10] T. S. Eliot, *Letters of T. S. Eliot*, vol. 1, ed. Valerie Eliot (New York: Harcourt Brace Jovanovich, 1988), 26.
[11] James E. Miller, Jr., *T. S. Eliot: The Making of an American Poet, 1888–1922* (University Park, PA: Pennsylvania State University Press, 2005), 118.
[12] Eliot, *Letters*, 43–44.

embraced a comprehensive idea of Europe rather than any national identity, and he adhered to this commitment throughout his career.[13] Despite the bitter divisiveness of the First World War, in "Tradition and the Individual Talent" (1919) Eliot advised the aspiring poet to become familiar with the "mind of Europe" as well as the "mind of his own country."[14] In the first issue of the *Criterion* in 1922, Eliot included Hermann Hesse's essay on "Recent German Poetry." European culture—past and present, French and German—was Eliot's lodestone.

Like others of his generation, Eliot came to Expressionism via Symbolism. He discovered avant-garde poetry through Arthur Symons's turn-of-the-century book about Symbolism and spoke of this event as if it were a religious epiphany: "if we can recall the time when we were ignorant of the French symbolists, and met with *The Symbolist Movement in Literature*, we remember that book as an introduction to wholly new feelings, as a revelation."[15] He became Laforgue's disciple: "I remember getting hold of Laforgue years ago at Harvard, purely through reading Symons.... I do feel more grateful to him than to anyone else, and I do not think that I have come across any other

---

[13] See Leon Surette, *Dreams of a Totalitarian Utopia: Literary Modernism and Politics* (Montreal: McGill-Queen's University Press, 2011). Surette argues that Eliot probably first read Charles Maurras in 1911 but never adopted Maurras's nationalism. Although Eliot "clung to the Action Française fantasies of a Christian, Royalist polity" (161), his vision of "pan-Europeanism" was a constant in his career (185), and it was responsible for deterring him from fascism: "Eliot's Arnoldian instincts led him toward a 'European' culture—as opposed to a British, French, German, or Italian—so it was natural for him to choose trans-nationalism as the carrot to draw Europeans toward Christianity. Hitler's instincts were the reverse" (260).

[14] T. S. Eliot, "Tradition and the Individual Talent," in *Selected Essays* (New York: Harcourt, Brace & World, Inc., 1964), 6.

[15] T. S. Eliot, "The Perfect Critic," in *The Sacred Wood* (London: Methuen, 1950), 5.

writer since who has meant so much to me as he did at that particular moment, or that particular year."[16]

Although Eliot called attention to French poets, Symons considered Symbolism a European phenomenon. Dedicating his book to W. B. Yeats as the chief Symbolist writing in English, Symons explained that he had focused on French literature only because "France is the country of movements."[17] "In Germany," he observed, Symbolism "seems to be permeating the whole of literature" (v). Since Symbolism posited that "the visible world is no longer a reality, and the unseen world no longer a dream" (4), it provided an alternative to religious versions of nonempirical experience. This belief in the power of art to provide access to transcendent meaning did not last.

After the turn of the century, artists and writers in Central Europe continued the Symbolist fight against materialism, but they were less certain of victory. Unable to discover an "unseen world" beyond visible reality, they sought meaning in subjective experience. Laforgue himself illustrates how Symbolist aims could lead to Expressionist means. Although his poems project the persona of a cynical sophisticate who ridicules bourgeois ideals, he cannot stifle the intense feelings characteristic of Expressionism. Symons hears strains of self-pity (108) in Laforgue's "balanced, chill, colloquial style" (105). Graham Dunstan Martin, the editor of Laforgue's *Selected Poems*, also finds self-pity beneath the irony.[18] He notes that Laforgue's contemporary Jacques Rivière, reputed

---

[16] Eliot, *Letters*, 191.

[17] Symons, *Symbolist Movement*, (v).

[18] Graham Dunstan Martin, "Introduction," *Selected Poems: Jules Laforgue* (New York: Penguin, 1998), xii.

to be "a great literary opinion-former," thought that Laforgue was "*pleurard et pédant*' (snivelling and over-learned)" (xiii). Rivière was the secretary of *La Nouvelle Revue Française*, which had been founded in 1909 to publish post-Symbolist writers.[19] Since Rivière was the brother-in-law of Eliot's friend Alain–Fournier, Eliot might have heard such negative opinions of Laforgue while in France. For Symons and Rivière, Laforgue was less a detached *flâneur* than a latent Expressionist.

Expressionism absorbed the antimaterialist aim of Symbolism but was far more turbulent. The art historian Peter Selz describes Expressionism in terms that echo Symons's account of Symbolism as a response to religious doubts: the "expressionist movement may be seen in part as a reaction against the prevailing values of the deceptively stable society in which the artists grew up. In their reaction against materialism and rationalism they were attempting to affirm the values of the spiritual. Frequently they turned to religious subjects, or used art as a spiritual substitute for religion."[20] But Selz emphasizes a difference in tone that indicates a new attitude: "Frequently, where symbolism merely suggests and understates, expressionism exaggerates and overstates" (64). This intensity prevents Expressionism from performing the "sacred ritual" that Symons values in Symbolism. As Thomas Harrison argues in *1910: The Emancipation of Dissonance*, "Expressionist art expresses more of the tension than the unity of ecstatic experience. Where ecstasy is presented as mystical union or transport we have symbolism

---

[19] Miller, *Making of an American Poet*, 118.
[20] Peter Selz, *German Expressionist Painting* (Berkeley and Los Angeles: University of California Press, 1957), viii.

rather than expressionism."[21] Harrison's distinction emphasizes the subjective orientation of Expressionism.

Extremes of emotion ranging from self-pity and erotic desire to outrage at injustice are felt subjectively, even though external conditions cause these feelings. Kurt Pinthus, an early supporter of Expressionist poetry, recalled that "the over-stimulated and over-sensitive nerves and souls of the poets were already clearly perceiving on the one side the dull advance of the proletarian masses robbed of love and joy, and from the other side the imminent collapse of a humanity that was as arrogant as it was indifferent."[22] Their poems registered the inner effect of external events. For this generation, ordinary life was unbearable. Lower-class ugliness and upper-class emptiness were equally contemptible, and no vocation seemed worth pursuing.

Young people blamed their distress on social disorder. They saw signs of a secular apocalypse wherever they looked. For example, in "*Weltende*" (End of the World), written by Jakob van Hoddis in 1911, both catastrophic and mundane events are portents of disaster:

The burgher's hat flies off his pointed head,

Everywhere the air reverberates with what sounds like screams.

Roofers are falling off and breaking in two,

And along the coasts—the paper says—the tide is rising.

---

[21] Thomas Harrison, *1910: The Emancipation of Dissonance* (Berkeley, Los Angeles, London: University of California Press, 1996), 203.

[22] Kurt Pinthus, ed., *Menschheitsdämmerung, Dawn of Humanity: A Document of Expressionism*, trans. Joanna M. Ratych, Ralph Ley, and Robert C. Conard (Columbia, SC: Camden House, 1994), 32.

The storm is here, the wild seas are hopping....

Most people have a cold.

The trains are dropping off the bridges. (61)

This poem came to characterize the movement.[23] Its juxtaposition of disparate images was known as *Reihungsstil* (paratactical style) or *Simultangedicht* (simultaneous poem).[24] The incongruity of the images is ironic, yet it also signifies that danger is ubiquitous. The poem is an example of Neil H. Donahue's observation that "Expressionist subject matter seems to fluctuate wildly between the antipodes of rural idyll and metropolitan alienation, between tranquility and catastrophe...."[25] The same formal and thematic characteristics appear in Eliot's early poems. The parallels between losing a hat and falling off a roof, between a cold and a train wreck, resemble Eliot's use of parataxis to locate ominous meanings in ordinary things, as in "Goldfish":

And the waltzes turn, return,

Float and fall,

Like the cigarettes

Of our marionettes,

Inconsequent, intolerable.[26]

Even the "inconsequent" is "intolerable."

[23] Klaus Weissenberger, "Performing the Poem: Rituals of Activism in Expressionist Poetry," in *A Companion to the Literature of German Expressionism*, ed. Neil H. Donahue (Rochester, NY: Camden House, 2005), 187.

[24] Francis Michael Sharp, "*Menschheitsdämmerung*: The Aging of a Canon," in *A Companion to the Literature of German Expressionism*, ed. Neil H. Donahue (Rochester, NY: Camden House, 2005), 139.

[25] Neil H. Donahue, "Introduction," in *A Companion to the Literature of German Expressionism*, ed. Neil H. Donahue (Rochester, NY: Camden House, 2005), 12.

[26] T. S. Eliot, *Inventions of the March Hare*, ed. Christopher Ricks (New York: Harcourt Brace & Company, 1996), 26.

Similarly, in "Prufrock's Pervigilium" ordinary things portend disaster. Dawn spreads not light but a miasma:

And when the dawn at length had realized itself
And turned with a sense of nausea, to see what it had stirred ...

After a night of insomnia, the speaker imagines his world collapsing:

I fumbled to the window to experience the world
And to hear my Madness singing, sitting on the kerbstone
[A blind old drunken man who sings and mutters,
With broken boot heels stained in many gutters]
And as he sang the world began to fall apart ... (43)

The speaker has seen "the world roll up into a ball/Then suddenly dissolve and fall away" (44). By the end of the poem, he is no longer alone. The plural pronoun of the opening lines returns: "Till human voices wake us, and we drown" (46). Like van Hoddis, Eliot writes about life as if the world is ending.

Pinthus chose *"Weltende"* as the opening poem in his 1919 anthology *Menschheitsdämmerung* (Dawn of Humanity), which has been credited with defining the Expressionist canon.[27] He organized his selection of poems as a "symphony" in four movements to demonstrate the range of themes, moods, and forms in Expressionism (28). The ambiguity of *dämmerung*, which means "half-light,"

---

[27] Pinthus, *Menschheitsdämmerung*, 60. In his 1971 introduction to a new edition, "The History of *Menschheitsdämmerung*," Pinthus cites a later tribute to the importance of the anthology: "Kurt Batt, one of East Germany's most recognized critics, not only calls *Menschheitsdämmerung* an 'exemplary selection of characteristic poems worth handing down,' but proclaims: 'The fame and influence of this literary movement were based, not least, on *Menschheitsdämmerung*; indeed, it may be seriously doubted whether without this anthology Expressionism would be seen as what it is in the consciousness of posterity.'"

and the tonal range of music are as significant in this collection as they are in Eliot's *March Hare* poems. Two of Eliot's "Preludes" have German titles that resemble the title of Pinthus's anthology: "Morgandämmerung" (Dawn) and "Abenddämmerung" (Dusk). Eliot's images of dusk convey intense but indistinct feelings as they do in Expressionism. As Russell E. Brown observes, Ernst Stadler, Georg Trakl, and Georg Heym use dusk as a general trope for personal and social decline.[28] The musical allusion of "Preludes" reprises Stadler's 1905 volume *Praeludien*, and the malaise in Eliot's poems fits Francis Michael Sharp's account of Expressionist discontent: "Characteristic of Heym's verse as well as Stadler's is a dissatisfaction and impatience with the staleness, the unheroic quality, and the lack of vitality in his times, a widely shared attitude that found popular expression in the enthusiasm that greeted the outbreak of the First World War."[29]

Eliot's poems voice similar complaints about everyday life. For example, in "Prelude in Dorchester (Houses)," written in 1910, residents of a modest neighborhood endure "The burnt-out ends of smoky days" as if their lives were as sordid as their surroundings.[30] The speaker in "First Caprice in North Cambridge" bemoans "The yellow evening flung against the panes/Of dirty windows" and the "Bottles and broken glass," yet he mocks the intensity of his reaction in the last line: "Oh, these minor considerations!" (13). Like his European counterparts, Eliot portrays a society that demands too much and offers too little.

This generation felt that its desires—aesthetic, erotic, and spiritual—were blocked at every turn. As Pinthus writes:

---

[28] Russell E. Brown, "Time of Day in Early Expressionist Poetry," *PMLA* 84 (1969): 27.
[29] Sharp, "Aging of a Canon," 143.
[30] Eliot, *March Hare*, 334.

The young people of this generation found themselves in a time from which every trace of ethos had disappeared.... The aggregate of hedonistically pleasurable things had to be as extensive and varied as possible; art was measured completely by an aesthetic yardstick, life completely by a materialistic, statistical yardstick; and the human being and his spiritual activity seemed only to exist in order to be observed psychologically, analytically, to be defined in accordance with historical maxims.[31]

Outrage at these conditions led to extreme protests. Gottfried Benn, the Expressionist poet most often compared to Eliot, recalled the violence of the poetic outcry: "A revolt with eruptions, ecstasies, hate, longing for a new humanity, with the dashing of language in order to dash the world...."[32] Similarly, Walter E. Sokel, in his classic study of Expressionism *The Writer in Extremis*, notes that poets emitted a "cataract of highly charged emotional words," suggesting the "apocalyptic extremity" of a "formless shriek."[33] This intensity is a fundamental element of Expressionism, though shrieking is not the only form it takes.

Artists and writers cast themselves as martyrs to their ideals. Harrison lists visual examples such as "Schiele's Saint Sebastian, Schoenberg's martyrs and haunted faces, Kokoschka's and Nolde's Christ—figures all nailed to a cross."[34] The figure of the secular martyr also appears in one of Eliot's miscellaneous quatrains:

---

[31] Pinthus, *Menschheitsdämmerung*, 31.

[32] Quoted in Pinthus, *Menschheitsdämmerung*, 13.

[33] Sokel, *In Extremis*, 111 and 4. One of his examples is Edvard Munch's 1893 painting "*Der Schrei*," an image of unmistakable emotion in a highly generalized time and place.

[34] Harrison, *1910*, 197.

He said: "this crucifixion was dramatic

He had not passed his life on officechairs

They did not crucify him in an attic

Up six abysmal flights of broken stairs."[35]

In "The Love Song of Saint Sebastian," which Eliot wrote while in Germany in 1914, martyrdom acquires erotic and sadomasochistic motives:

You would love me because I should have strangled you

And because of my infamy;

And I should love you the more because I had mangled you

And because you were no longer beautiful

To anyone but me. (78–79)[36]

While such imagery invites biographical interpretation, martyrs are so common in Expressionist art and writing that they begin to seem more conventional than confessional.

From the perspective of later events, the Expressionist response to bourgeois life may seem adolescent. As Eliot asks in "Fourth Caprice in Montparnasse":

Among such scattered thoughts as these

We turn the corner of the street;

But why are we so hard to please?[37]

---

[35] Eliot, *March Hare*, 71.

[36] See also Symons, *Symbolist Movement*, 156. His discussion of Maeterlinck's *Le Tragique Quotidien* mentions a similar example of erotic violence: "I have come to believe that this motionless old man lived really a more profound, human, and universal life than the lover who strangles his mistress, the captain who gains a victory, or the husband who 'avenges his honour.'"

[37] Eliot, *March Hare*, 14.

Unable to answer this question, the Expressionist generation represented its distress as disintegration. In *Theorizing the Avant-Garde*, Richard Murphy characterizes Expressionism in terms that fit "Prufrock": "the avant-garde text stages subjectivity as fragmented and discontinuous, for example as a constellation of personae, a series of mutually conflicting and contradictory roles played out by seemingly separate figures in the texts."[38] Nevertheless, Murphy excludes Eliot from the Expressionist avant-garde. Whereas Benn's "longing for a mythical order" was "problematized as a regressive and nostalgic turning-away from modernity" (102, n. 50), Murphy claims that Eliot believed in "the existence of a separate, transcendent and self-sufficient world of art" as a source of order (256–57, n. 16). In 1914, however, Eliot was as inclined to "parody" and "de-aestheticize" received ideas as anyone else in the avant-garde (256). When Prufrock says, "Let us go then, you and I," he could be walking through Berlin or Munich, manifesting the fragmented subjectivity Murphy describes.

Another Expressionist analogue for Prufrock is the Prodigal Son in Rainer Maria Rilke's novel *The Notebooks of Malte Laurids Brigge* (1910). Harrison interprets the parable of the Prodigal Son in relation to the Expressionist generation:

In Malte's version, the Prodigal Son is the story of a person who left home because he *did not want* to be loved. At home, where everyone doted on him, he was oppressed by a feeling that "most things were already decided," decided rhetorically, that is, within a system of familiar and reciprocal interest ... "one was the person

---

[38] Richard Murphy, *Theorizing the Avant-Garde: Modernism, Expressionism, and the Problem of Postmodernity* (Cambridge: Cambridge University Press, 1999), 18.

for whom they took one here; the person for whom, out of his little past and their own wishes, they had long fashioned a life."[39]

Such a life of domestic oppression, social rounds, and trivial decisions is the very situation that paralyzes Prufrock:

And I have known the eyes, I have known them all

The eyes that fix you in a formulated phrase

And when I am formulated sprawling on a pin

When I am pinned and wriggling on the wall,

Then how should I begin?

—To spit out all the butt ends of my days and ways?[40]

Prufrock, like the figures that Pinthus and Rilke portray, resents being objectified and measured, yet he is unable to show others that he is more than they perceive.

Sokel groups Eliot with German writers for whom "cerebralism" was "the chief existential problem": only "[a]esthetic cognition, the universe of memories and irony, saves them."[41] Sokel detects this Expressionist syndrome in Prufrock's wish that "he could be 'a pair of ragged claws/Scuttling across the floors of silent seas'" (96). Whereas Christopher Ricks's long notes for these lines mention sources as various as Darwin's *Descent of Man*, the "Crab Louse" associated with venereal disease, a scene involving crabs in Turgenev's *Smoke*, and *The Ancient Mariner*,[42] Sokel finds Prufrock's "longing for retrogression to a simpler, less inhibited way of life"

---

[39] Harrison, *1910*, 207.
[40] Eliot, *March Hare*, 40.
[41] Sokel, *In Extremis*, 119.
[42] Christopher Ricks, ed., *Inventions of the March Hare* (New York: Harcourt Brace & Company, 1996), 187–88.

characteristic of Expressionism.[43] The German context seems at least as relevant as Ricks's references. Like Sokel's examples of cerebral poets, Prufrock conveys the depth of his feelings by attempting to escape them. The lassitude of "And would it have been worth it, after all" defends against anxieties about mortality and mockery, which seem equally threatening: "And I have seen the eternal FOOTMAN hold my coat, and snicker—/And in short, I was afraid."[44] The servility of "Deferential, glad to be of use,/Politic, cautious, and meticulous" suggests suppressed ambition, while the self-deprecation of "Almost, at times, the Fool" (46) masks intellectual pride. Such feelings were not merely Eliot's; they were characteristic of the Expressionist generation.

Although Expressionist writing is often strident in its sincerity, it can also be ironic. Its extreme disparities between tone and implied feeling produce irony. James Rolleston perceives irony in Expressionism's effort to replace the individual lyric voice with a collective, "choric" presence. For example, "Benn speaks with an authentically choric, deindividualized consciousness, inspecting the still-smouldering ruins, but his tone is fundamentally ironic."[45] Rolleston also detects irony in Benn's use of "consciously hermetic" language (176), "fragmentation," and "citation" (179).[46] Although these qualities are commonly associated with postwar modernism, they first appear in prewar Expressionism and Eliot's early poems.

---

[43] Sokel, *In Extremis*, 96.

[44] Eliot, *March Hare*, 45.

[45] James Rolleston, "Choric Consciousness in Expressionist Poetry: Ernst Stadler, Else Lasker-Schüler, Georg Heym, Georg Trakl, Gottfried Benn," in *A Companion to the Literature of German Expressionism*, ed. Neil H. Donahue (Rochester, NY: Camden House, 2005), 176.

[46] See also Alfred Kubin, *The Other Side*, trans. Mike Mitchell (UK: Dedalus Ltd, 2000), 87. This dystopian novel written in 1908 is another example of Expressionist irony. The story is a fantasy of a "Dream Realm" that ends as a nightmare, not a nightmare of materialism

Calling attention to Eliot's affinities with Expressionist poets, Sokel notes the importance of irony to both Benn and Eliot:

This poetry is at once ironic and elegiac; and this combination, plus Alexandrian learning and musical artistry, relates Benn to Eliot, a kinship which Eliot acknowledged when he paraphrased Benn at length in his "Three Voices of Poetry." Like Eliot, Benn looks at the cultural-social reality of Western man in his period of decline and contemplates the constancies and contrasts, the eternal pattern of myth and the sterilized vulgarity of the technological era side by side.[47]

Benn's mockery of vulgar seduction in "*Nachtcafe*" (Night Café) (1912) resembles Eliot's use of derogatory physical descriptions and cheap urban settings to convey the degradation of modern life. In the third section of "Mandarins," Eliot demeans the entrenched elite:

The eldest of the mandarins,

A stoic in obese repose,

With intellectual double chins,

Regards the corner of his nose.[48]

Benn's synecdoches are more severe:

but of dissolution. Primarily a visual artist, Kubin was a member of Kandinsky's circle in Munich, and his novel satirizes avant-garde art as well as many other aspects of contemporary society. The narrator records his initial reaction to a potential rival, the artist Castringius: "Before I arrived Castringius had his simplest period. Three or four lines and the picture was finished. He called it 'Greatness'. His most important works had titles such as *The Head, He, She, Us, It!* They placed no limits on the imagination. For example, a head in a flower vase—it could mean anything." Kubin's irony targets the Expressionist use of abstraction to represent a spiritual essence purified of particulars. His narrator suggests that instead of everyone finding a common transcendent meaning, each viewer projects a personal interpretation. This critique, as Harrison shows, continues to shape debates about Expressionism. I am grateful to Marianne Thormählen for directing me to Kubin's novel.

[47] Sokel, *In Extremis*, 114.

[48] Eliot, *March Hare*, 21.

Young goitre is sweet on saddle-nose.

He treats her to three beers.

Sycosis buys carnations
to mollify double chin.

B minor: sonata op. 35.
A pair of eyes roars out:
Don't splash the blood of Chopin around the place
for this crowd to slouch about in![49]

In "Portrait of a Lady," Eliot also measures contemporary decline against Chopin:

We have been, let us say, to hear the latest Pole
Transmit the *Preludes*, through his hair and finger tips
"So intimate, this Chopin, that I think his soul
Should be resurrected only among friends
Some two or three, who will not touch the bloom
That is rubbed and questioned in the concert room"[50]

Just as Eliot irreverently compares the evening to a "patient etherized upon a table" in "Prufrock" (39), Benn describes a prank in a morgue in "Little Aster" (1912):

A drowned beer-truck driver was lifted on the slab.
Someone had stuck a dark-bright purple aster
between his teeth.[51]

---

[49] Gottfried Benn, "Night Café," trans. Michael Hamburger, in *Primal Vision: Selected Writings of Gottfried Benn*, ed. E. B. Ashton (New York: New Directions, 1971), 219.

[50] Eliot, *March Hare*, 327.

[51] Pinthus, *Menschheitsdämmerung*, 75.

The incongruous mixture of the serious and the trivial, and the sincere and the ironic, flouts decorum, undermining conventional standards of art and behavior.

The similarities between Eliot's early poems and Expressionism expand their significance. Instead of regarding the *March Hare* poems as sui generis hints of Eliot's postwar canon, we can see how they reflect a widespread cultural crisis. Although many examples of Expressionism seem to be the one-note *cri de coeur* of a solitary being, the movement was a generation's response to the collapse of the nineteenth-century's consensus of belief. As Benn wrote, "1910, that is indeed the year when all scaffolds began to crack."[52] Even the return of Halley's Comet that year seemed to give cosmic validation to anxieties about collective "doom and degeneration" (2). Neither Expressionism nor Eliot's poems were merely private complaints.

In the wake of Symbolist claims that art was a secular substitute for religion, Expressionists also hoped to reveal a human essence that was inaccessible to sensory perception. The urgent need for alternatives to materialism led them to abstraction. Wassily Kandinsky, in his manifesto *Concerning the Spiritual in Art* (1912), diagnosed the same crisis of belief that others perceived at this time:

> Our minds, which are even now only just awakening after years of materialism, are infected with the despair of unbelief, of lack of purpose and ideal. The nightmare of materialism, which has turned the life of the universe into an evil, useless game, is not yet past; it holds the awakening soul still in its grip.[53]

---

[52] Quoted in Harrison, *1910*, 1.
[53] Wassily Kandinsky, *Concerning the Spiritual in Art*, trans. M. T. H. Sadler (New York: Dover Publications, 1977), 1–2.

The usual remedies for this infection were no longer effective: "When religion, science and morality are shaken, the two last by the strong hand of Nietzsche, and when the outer supports threaten to fall, man turns his gaze from externals in onto himself" (14). Kandinsky thought that art was a cure for the nightmare of materialism and the aimlessness of secularity. Art provided "material expressions of the soul" (41) in response to "the inner need" (35). Whereas Symbolists posited correspondences between the visible and invisible, Kandinsky claimed that abstraction was the way to represent spiritual meaning. His aesthetic principle was that the "more obvious is the separation from nature, the more likely is the inner meaning to be pure and unhampered" (50). Distorting empirical reality was a way to convey "the 'inner' by way of the 'outer'" (17). Like many other Expressionists, he believed that music, more than other arts, approached this ideal: "A painter, who finds no satisfaction in mere representation, however artistic, in his longing to express his inner life, cannot but envy the ease with which music, the most non-material of the arts today, achieves this end" (19). He alluded to musical forms by giving paintings titles like *Improvisation* and *Composition*.[54]

Comparing Kandinsky and Arnold Schoenberg, Harrison argues that by 1910 two kinds of Expressionist art had emerged:

If the Munich school of Kandinsky and Marc gives an intellectual, metaphysical face to this self-expressive discord, painters in Vienna, Dresden, and later Berlin are more struck by the toll it takes on the psyche. Schoenberg is as pivotal a figure here as he is in Munich.... While his atonal music is analogous to the

---

[54] Selz, *German Expressionist Painting*, 205.

abstractions of Munich, his pictorial work, is closer to the tortured figural representations produced in other Germanic cities.[55]

Harrison formulates the paradox of subjective feeling leading to impersonal knowledge in relation to Schoenberg's *The Red Gaze* (1910). As in many other Expressionist paintings, wide-open, staring eyes dominate a disembodied face with indistinct features. Harrison asks, "What is the affliction from which his face suffers? Is it personal or communal in nature?" (1). Harrison's answer is that a communal crisis of belief caused "that new twentieth-century emotion called angst—as ancient, no doubt, as existence itself, but collectively perceptible only in the new cultural conditions" (111). Schoenberg's tormented face may seem far more personal than Kandinsky's vague shapes and colors, but both painters reflect the Expressionist assumption that subjective experience is the source of impersonal meaning. To meet the spiritual needs of a secular culture, Kandinsky and other Expressionists cut away the incidentals of personality to expose an impersonal core. Responding to the demise of religious faith, artists tried to represent inner meaning.

Whether striving for universal spirituality like Kandinsky's abstractions or evoking contemporary angst like Schoenberg's martyrs, the movement was unrelentingly subjective. Pinthus includes both personal and impersonal forms of this subjectivity in the four symphonic movements of his anthology. Poems about private feelings appear in "Crash and Cry" and "Awakening of the Heart," and poems about communal bonds appear in "Call-to-Action and Revolt" and "Love to Human Beings." In a 1959 commentary,

---

[55] Harrison, *1910*, 60.

Pinthus attributes the characteristic intensity of both kinds of poems to social forces:

> And time and again it must be said that the quality of this poetry rests in its intensity. Never before in world literature did there resonate as loudly, piercingly, and stirringly cry, crash, and longing of an age as from the wild band of these forerunners and martyrs, whose hearts were pierced not by the romantic arrows of Amor or Eros but by the tortures of an accursed youth, a detested society, the murderous years they were forced to endure.[56]

Sounding the theme of martyrdom, he indicts society for the "tortures of an accursed youth." Although the pain was felt individually, poets claimed that it had a communal meaning:

> Thus social aspects are not presented in realistic detail, are not depicted objectively as, e.g., slum art (like the kind in vogue around 1890), but they are always totally directed toward the universal, toward the great ideas of humanity. (35)

The assumption that subjective experience could reveal universal experience led to forms that were highly individualized yet abstract.

Like Pinthus, Sokel emphasizes the subjective foundation of both intellectual and emotional types of Expressionism: "Expressionism as abstract form, as part of the modernist movement, and Expressionism as formless shriek, arise from the same factor—subjectivism."[57] He notes that in addition to the more familiar "fundamental qualities and devices of Expressionism—the tense urgency, the extremism and

---

[56] Pinthus, *Menschheitsdämmerung*, 36.
[57] Sokel, *In Extremis*, 4.

violence, the need for the outcry, for the breathless condensation, the hectic hyperbole, the metaphoric visualization" (226), some poets "developed the possibilities of linguistic condensation and abstraction" (111). Herwarth Walden, who founded *Der Sturm* in Berlin in 1910, presented Expressionism as a "'view of the world (*Weltanschauung*).'"[58] H. Stefan Schultz explains: "Expressionism is the intellectual movement of a time which places the inner experience above external life. But this inner experience is not personal; the artist is the involuntary (blind) servant of the 'Never experienced'" (13–14). Claiming that the intensity of feeling in Expressionism transcends the individual poet, Walden accounts for the impersonal aim of subjective art.

Eliot also takes up the question that Harrison poses: Does Expressionism portray private anguish or communal angst, a psychological condition or a social situation? Eliot's answer appears in "Tradition and the Individual Talent" (1919). By balancing subjective feeling and public meaning, Eliot asserts, "Poetry is not a turning loose of emotion, but an escape from emotion; it is not the expression of personality, but an escape from personality. But, of course, only those who have personality and emotions know what it means to want to escape from these things."[59] This definition of poetry is almost identical to Sokel's description of Expressionism: "The continuous personality of the artist, his experiences, his individuality, his 'soul' command no interest. The artist is to be nothing more than an executive organ for the record production

---

[58] H. Stefan Schultz, "German Expressionism: 1905–1925," *Chicago Review* 13 (1959): 13.
[59] Eliot, "Tradition and the Individual Talent," 10–11.

[*sic*] of works."[60] For Expressionists, sensory perception was merely a source of objective knowledge, useful for discerning physical distinctions; only subjective feelings and thoughts could reveal underlying commonalities among individuals. In this context, Eliot's assertion that the "emotion of art is impersonal" is more theoretical than self-protective.[61] His sardonic aside that "only those who have personality and emotions know what it means to want to escape from these things" perfectly states the Expressionist conviction that the source of both personal and impersonal meaning was subjective. Whether Expressionist form was abstract or distorted, the tone sincere or ironic, the goal was not to give vent to personal feelings, but to reveal a fundamental human essence. Since this essence was thought to be inaccessible to empirical examination, poets turned inward, assuming that subjectivity produced impersonal knowledge.

After the war, the aesthetic current shifted from Expressionist subjectivity to Post-Expressionist objectivity, carrying Eliot along with it. Reacting against spiritual justifications for the war, people came to distrust appeals to inner experience as a source of social unity. To reduce the ambiguity of indistinct and abstract forms, the postwar movement called New Objectivity (also known as Magic Realism) attempted to ground meanings in particular cultural settings. This change is apparent in the contrast between the prewar abstraction of Kandinsky and the postwar specificity of George Grosz, Otto Dix, and Christian Schad. Although the later paintings are not realistic, they refer to a recognizable world.

---

[60] Sokel, *In Extremis*, 106.
[61] Eliot, "Tradition and the Individual Talent," 11.

The differences between "Prufrock" and *The Waste Land* register the impact of the war in a similar way. Eliot replaced the subjective perspective of a single speaker in "Prufrock" with a wide range of cultural voices. The speakers of *The Waste Land* are presented objectively as distinct individuals tied to particular social positions.[62] In *A Genealogy of Modernism*, Michael Levenson links the poem to its era in terms that illustrate Taylor's conception of secularity.[63] Levenson notes the absence of a consistent point of view (190), the use of parallels in place of narrative (200), and the "anthropological temper which understands by comparing, which sets systems of belief in relation to one another, and which disallows the special claims of any single system" (202). As he shows, "In *The Waste Land* Eliot acknowledges the greatest range of attitudes and faiths, with the consequence that none comes to final dominance" (202).[64] The poem switches between aristocratic and common speakers and literary and colloquial language without transitions. We hear *Tristan and Isolde*, music hall songs, and the Upanishads. The incongruous juxtaposition

---

[62] See Valerie Eliot, ed., *The Waste Land. A Facsimile and Transcript of the Original Drafts Including the Annotations of Ezra Pound* (New York: Harcourt Brace Jovanovich, Inc., 1971), 1. The epigraph states that Eliot later regarded *The Waste Land* as a "piece of rhythmical grumbling" that he had written to relieve "a personal and wholly insignificant grouse against life." Eliot's self-deprecating remark is consistent with the relationship between private feeling and public experience articulated in Expressionist texts and "Tradition and the Individual Talent."

[63] Michael Levenson, *A Genealogy of Modernism: A Study of English Literary Doctrine, 1908-1922* (Cambridge: Cambridge University Press, 1984), 165–211.

[64] Levenson also points out the ironic strategies of Eliot's shorter poems: "The strong accents, the unlikely rhymes, the rapid movement of thought, the casual appropriation of a cultural past, these are devices well suited to the methods of irony, and if the quatrain form represents a 'precise way of thinking and feeling' for Eliot, it is the way of irony—not the incidental ironies of 'Prufrock,' but irony as the structural principle of the whole.... These poems are built out of certain violent contrasts...and their development consists in the unfolding of stark antitheses" (161). These characteristics also appear in *The Waste Land*.

of characters, quotations, tones, discourses, and images generates irony and destabilizes meaning. Having assimilated the angst of his generation before the war, Eliot later joined his cohort's return to empirical reality, tethering postwar feelings to specific circumstances. In contrast, the single speaker of "Prufrock" has a consistent voice. Quotation marks indicate when he is quoting someone else, and his identity and situation are generalized. The use of metaphor, allusion, and discursive reflection rather than speech makes the speaker's subjectivity seem impersonal.

Eliot's early poems are statements of social angst as well as private anguish. "Prufrock" and the other *March Hare* poems are legible as part of the Expressionist movement. The similarities between the *March Hare* poems and Expressionism substantiate Eliot's claim in "Tradition and the Individual Talent" that no poet "has his complete meaning alone."[65] While the spiritual yearning in these poems may anticipate his later religious faith, this longing is part of the Expressionist generation's quest for secular meaning. While the extreme images of the early poems may be signs of sexual repression, his emotional turmoil resembles that of other young men throughout Europe who were unwilling to conform to social expectations. Rejecting the religious and political beliefs of their elders, they sought meaning within themselves, but like Eliot, they soon found that they needed more than inner knowledge to create art about contemporary life. In the context of the European avant-garde, the subjectivity of Eliot's early poetry is part of his generation's search for impersonal meaning in emotion. He did not turn to art as an escape from social disruption but as a way to reveal it.

---

[65] Eliot, "Tradition and the Individual Talent," 4.

3

D. H. Lawrence's *Women in Love* and men at war

D. H. Lawrence wrote the first version of *Women in Love* in 1916, the year of the battles of Verdun and the Somme, yet the text never refers to the war directly. As a result, critics disagree about the depth of Lawrence's engagement in contemporary events. But if we compare the novel to other aesthetic responses to the war, the political dimension of the text is unmistakable. After eloping with Frieda von Richthofen in 1912, Lawrence was immersed in European avant-garde culture, and this contact with new ideas about politics, economics, sexuality, psychology, and art changed his writing. He adopted the Expressionist use of abstraction to convey subjective experience, and after 1914 he joined the Post-Expressionist reaction. Like his European counterparts, Lawrence continued to seek inner meaning, but located it in recognizable settings. The formal transition from *The Rainbow* to *Women in Love* registers the impact of the war. Although both texts are symbolic, *Women in Love* provides much more information about its social context. This combination of symbolism and realism justifies Keith Sagar's claim that *Women in Love* was the first modernist novel in English.[1]

---

[1] Keith Sagar, *D. H. Lawrence's Paintings* (London: Chaucer Press, 2003), 19.

The Expressionist elements of *The Rainbow* have been described in detail by Jack F. Stewart, Henry Schvey, and others, but the resemblance between Post-Expressionism and *Women in Love* has received less attention, partly because the styles of the two novels are often conflated.[2] Although Lawrence originally planned a single narrative titled "The Wedding Ring" about several generations of the Brangwen family, he split the manuscript into two parts and emphasized the contrast between them. In 1916, he told his agent that he was writing "a sequel to the *Rainbow*, though quite unlike it."[3] In 1917, Lawrence described the first part of the Brangwen saga as a "pre-war statement," whereas the second "actually does contain the results in one's soul of the war."[4] The subtitle for the 1916 draft was "Dies Irae" (Day of Wrath and Last Judgment),[5] and the 1919 foreword to the revised text explicitly connects the personal conflicts in the novel to public events: the "bitterness of the war may be taken for granted in the characters" (485). "We are now in a period of crisis," Lawrence explains. "Every man who is acutely alive is acutely wrestling with his own soul" (486). This individual struggle has social consequences: "The people that can bring forth the new passion, the new idea, this people will endure" (486). Lawrence speaks of a people rather than a nation, and *Women in Love* attempts to do more than examine the immediate conflict

---

[2] See Jack F. Stewart, "Expressionism in *The Rainbow*," *Novel* 13 (1980): 296–315; Henry Schvey, "Lawrence and Expressionism," in *D. H. Lawrence: New Studies*, ed. Christopher Heywood (London: Macmillan, 1987), 125. Schvey finds Expressionism in both *The Rainbow* and *Women in Love*.

[3] D. H. Lawrence, *Letters of D. H. Lawrence*, vol. 2, ed. George J. Zytaruk and James T. Boulton (Cambridge: Cambridge University Press, 1981), 606.

[4] D. H. Lawrence, *Letters of D. H. Lawrence*, vol. 3, ed. James T. Boulton and Andrew Robertson (Cambridge: Cambridge University Press, 1984), 142–43.

[5] D. H. Lawrence, *Women in Love*, ed. David Farmer, Lindeth Vasey, and John Worthen (Cambridge: Cambridge University Press, 1987), xxxi.

between Germany and Great Britain by analyzing causes of aggression between individuals and groups. He aligns lovers' oscillating feelings with generational, class, and national confrontations.

Despite Lawrence's statements, critics dispute the social significance of violence in the novel. While some consider the personal relationships in the text to be an escape from public life, others regard them as symbols of political conflict. One of the most emphatic examples of the first position is Joyce Carol Oates's sweeping claim, "In Lawrence's work one is struck repeatedly by the total absence of concern for community."[6] She adds, "The human instinct for something larger than an intense, intimate bond, the instinct for community, is entirely absent in Lawrence, and this absence helps to account for the wildness of his characters' emotions" (32). Michael Squires casts this isolation in a positive light, arguing that the novel's violence "abstracts characters from history; puts them in closer, elemental touch with their being; and offers them the chance of renewal even though, paradoxically, renewal may devastate the existing order and its human relationships."[7] Taking the opposite position, Mark Kinkead-Weekes interprets the text as social critique: "Indeed, one of the most important things about *Women in Love* is that it is a war novel, even though its society is apparently at peace and its date left deliberately vague."[8] In his view, the personal

---

[6] Joyce Carol Oates, "Lawrence's *Götterdämmerung*: The Tragic Vision of *Women in Love*," in *D. H. Lawrence's "Women in Love*," ed. David Ellis (Oxford: Oxford University Press, 2006), 31.

[7] Michael Squires, "Modernism and the Contours of Violence in D. H. Lawrence's Fiction," *Studies in the Novel* 39 (2007): 93.

[8] Mark Kinkead-Weekes, "Violence in *Women in Love*," in *D. H. Lawrence's "Women in Love*," ed. David Ellis (Oxford: Oxford University Press, 2006), 223.

violence in the novel symbolizes public events: "For violence—now unmistakably physical and potentially lethal—wells up in most of the characters. Though Lawrence wished to trace its sources in a world apparently at peace, he clearly saw something apocalyptic about what had happened to his world in the year of the Somme and Verdun" (223).

John Worthen complicates the critical debate by arguing that the 1916 version, published as *The First 'Women in Love'*, reflects the historical moment, but the 1921 text does not:

> The 1916 *First 'Women in Love'* is a war novel to a much greater extent than the 1921 text; in part because one reads it differently, as the work of 1916, and in part because some passages which were subsequently cut, or changed, bore very heavily on the world of 1916–17 and would have struck 1917 readers with particular force.[9]

Worthen believes that the later version was overly influenced by Lawrence's reading of James Pryse and Madame Blavatsky (62), making it more metaphysical and less contemporary: "Even when Ursula sings so that Gudrun can do eurhythmic movements, in the 1916 novel she incongruously comes up with 'It's a long long way to Tipperary,' that most famous of wartime marching songs: it would have been hard to locate the novel more precisely in wartime (the song had only been published in 1912). None of these examples survived into the 1921 novel" (71).[10] Another example that does not appear in the later text is Birkin's final affirmation, "All is not

---

[9] John Worthen, "The First 'Women in Love,'" in *D. H. Lawrence's "Women in Love,"* ed. David Ellis (Oxford: Oxford University Press, 2006), 68–69.
[10] In the 1921 text Ursula sings the chorus to "My Gal is a High Born Lady." In Ken Russell's film adaptation, the song is changed yet again to the 1918 hit "I'm Forever Blowing Bubbles."

lost, because many are lost. —I am not afraid or ashamed to die and be dead."[11] Although Worthen points out that "many" includes soldiers, he argues that Birkin separates himself from them: "In 1917, of course, this could only have been read as a direct reference to the war, and to its dreadful losses, with Birkin attempting to stand clear and see differently."[12] Interpreting Birkin's words as a turning away from the "many" rather than as an identification with them, Worthen concludes that Lawrence withdraws from public life: "the 1917 reader would be getting a very clear signal: the larger stage of war and politics is here reduced to the purely personal stage—and peace is the greatest reality" (61). But Worthen's assumptions about the 1917 reader do not fit the artists and writers who had been part of the prewar avant-garde. They took the opposite path, moving from subjective angst to public anger. Lawrence was able to anticipate this turn because of his extended visits to Frieda's family in Germany.

Despite the diversity of styles Expressionism encompassed, artists were united in their opposition to conventions and criteria of the past. To publicize their aims, they formed various alliances, including *Der Blaue Reiter*, a group that Wassily Kandinsky organized with Franz Marc. Frieda's brother-in-law Edgar Jaffe owned a painting by Marc, and Kinkead-Weekes argues, "We do not know which *Blaue Reiter* painting by Franz Marc hung on Edgar Jaffe's wall, but DHL would almost certainly have seen, in 1912 or 1913, paintings imbued with Kandinsky's idea that the artist should try to show the forces within things, rather than their appearance—paintings such as Marc's *Blue*

---

[11] D. H. Lawrence, *The First 'Women in Love,'* ed. John Worthen and Lindeth Vasey (Cambridge: Cambridge University Press, 1998), 443.
[12] Worthen, "First *'Women in Love,'*" 68.

Horses (1911)."[13] Excluded from established venues, Expressionists presented their work in a series of "Secession" exhibitions. The second and final *Blaue Reiter* exhibition was held in Munich in 1912, just before Lawrence's first visit. He described the emotional intensity of this work with self-conscious irony in "Christs in the Tyrol," written the same year:

> I, who see a tragedy in every cow, began by suffering from the Secession pictures in Munich. All these new paintings seemed so shrill and restless. Those that were meant for joy shrieked and pranced for joy, and sorrow was a sensation to be relished, curiously; as if we were epicures in suffering, keen on a new flavour.[14]

Although his tone is facetious, Lawrence admired these pictures and developed a literary version of visual abstraction to represent intense feelings.

Expressionist artists gathered in the Schwabing district of Munich, but the other pole of avant-garde activity in Germany was in Heidelberg. Kinkead-Weekes notes that as a guest of Else and Edgar Jaffe, Lawrence would have become familiar not only with Munich Expressionists but also with "the opposite culture of Heidelberg and its new rational and social-scientific enlightenment, centred now on the Webers and particularly Max."[15] As Lawrence wrote in 1913, "We sit by lamplight and drink beer, and hear Edgar on Modern

---

[13] Mark Kinkead-Weekes, *D. H. Lawrence: Triumph to Exile, 1912–1922* (Cambridge: Cambridge University Press, 1996), 804, n. 88.
[14] D. H. Lawrence, "Christs in the Tyrol," in *Twilight in Italy and Other Essays*, ed. Paul Eggert (Cambridge: Cambridge University Press, 1994), 43.
[15] Kinkead-Weekes, *Triumph to Exile*, 39.

Capitalism. *Why* was I born?"[16] On another visit, Lawrence received a personal tutorial from Alfred Weber:

> finishing up with Exhibitions in Bern—and now I am with Prof Weber in Heidelberg hearing the latest things in German philosophy and political economy. I am like a little half fledged bird opening my beak *Very* wide to gulp down the fat phrases. But it is all very interesting. (186)

Introduced to current ideas in social science, Lawrence saw how theorists derived meaning from empirical data. These lessons supplemented what he learned from Expressionist representations of intense feeling.

Although Kinkead-Weekes documents the extent of Lawrence's exposure to prewar German culture, he argues that Lawrence's new work was "opposed both to emotional Expressionism and to rational Enlightenment, as merely different modes of self-importance and irreverence."[17] In contrast, I am arguing that Lawrence's time in Germany caused his writing to embrace both poles. His use of symbolic cues such as rhythm, repetition, and extremity creates a verbal version of the visual abstraction in Expressionist paintings. Oskar Kokoschka's *Bride of the Wind* (1913) and Marc's many paintings of horses could serve as illustrations for *The Rainbow*. When the war pulled artists away from subjective themes, Lawrence developed a style comparable to the more objective postwar paintings of artists such as Otto Dix, George Grosz, and Christian Schaad. While Expressionists suppressed outer appearance in favor of inner

---

[16] Lawrence, *Letters*, vol. 2, 63.
[17] Kinkead-Weekes, *Triumph to Exile*, 40.

meaning, after the war Lawrence and other Post-Expressionists wanted to connect them.

In *Rites of Spring*, the cultural historian Modris Eksteins argues that the embrace of material reality in postwar art was a reaction against everything associated with the prewar period, its materialism as well as the avant-garde critique of materialism. Eksteins demonstrates that in the first decades of the century spiritual unity had been a national preoccupation in Germany. The public embraced "symbol and myth" as the "essence of existence."[18] This contempt for everyday life in the name of "*eine innere Notwendigkeit*, a spiritual necessity" was manipulated to stir enthusiasm for the war (92). In Germany, the war "was a quest for authenticity, for truth, for self-fulfillment, for those values, that is, which the avant-garde had evoked prior to the war and against those features—materialism, banality, hypocrisy, tyranny—which it had attacked" (92). A number of Expressionist artists welcomed war as a "powerful catharsis" and volunteered for military service.[19] They wanted to destroy the "oppressive" order of the past and believed that "a better society would arise from its ruins" (13). The actual experience of war, however, transformed the idea of destruction into reality, and many of these artists repudiated their prewar aims and styles. Avant-garde artists were still concerned with meaning, but they were suspicious of free-floating ideas and emotions.

This change is evident in Lawrence's style as well. The spiritual intensity of prewar art dominates *The Rainbow*, especially in its

---

[18] Modris Eksteins, *Rites of Spring: The Great War and the Birth of the Modern Age* (Boston: Houghton Mifflin, 1989), 77.
[19] Dietmar Elger, *Expressionism: A Revolution in German Art* (Köln: Taschen, 2002), 13.

early chapters. From the great flood that kills Tom Brangwen to the closing image of the rainbow, the text evokes a visionary alternative to empirical reality. In contrast, both versions of *Women in Love* are more fully embedded in a particular social milieu. As in Post-Expressionist art, there are more specific references to the material world. We know what characters wear, how their hair is cut, where they live, how their rooms are furnished, what they eat, and the names of songs they sing. These details are the realistic foundation of symbolic scenes such as Birkin rolling in the grass at Breadalby, Gudrun dancing before the Highland cattle at Shortlands, and Birkin throwing stones at the reflection of the moon in a lake.

Although critics familiar with German culture usually consider both novels Expressionist, they also recognize the contrast between *The Rainbow* and *Women in Love*. For example, N. U. Seeber in "D. H. Lawrence, German Expressionism, and Weberian Formal Rationality" claims that Lawrence "aims at a spiritual renewal and awakening" in his readers and shares Expressionists' "preference for exotic and erotic motifs and, in form and the aesthetics of production, a peculiar dialectic of regression and abstraction."[20] Seeber argues that the apocalyptic ending of *The Rainbow* reflects the Expressionist tendency "to see the salvation of humanity merely in the total overthrow of all existing orders" (241). Seeber also finds these qualities in *Women in Love*, interpreting the "eschatological symbolism at the end of *Women in Love*" as a visionary order that fills the void left by the demise of the old world (240). He regards Gerald's death as "an expressionist vision

---

[20] N. U. Seeber, "D. H. Lawrence, German Expressionism, and Weberian Formal Rationality," *Miscelánea* 20 (1999): 237–39.

of horror and final things *par excellence*" and interprets the structure of the two sisters' relationships as a "characteristically expressionist schematic configuration" that "underwrites that allegory in which the will-to-power of the instrumental reason drives towards death, in contrast to the life-affirming, organicist mysticism represented by Rupert Birkin" (246). Read as an Expressionist text, *Women in Love* seems as unconcerned with the external world as Joyce Carol Oates claims.

Nevertheless, Seeber and others recognize a new interest in empirical reality in *Women in Love*. Seeber notes that Gerald's management philosophy implements the theories of contemporary sociologists such as Max Weber and Edgar Jaffe (247): "the authority with which Lawrence writes of social forms in *Women in Love* is reinforced by his acquaintance with the 'sociological ideas'...of Weber and cognate German thinkers, adding a depth and continuing relevance to his work which is missing from comparable expressionist texts" (251). Similarly, James Scott's 1979 article titled "'Continental': The Germanic Dimension of *Women in Love*" argues that references to Germany are not incidental but central to Lawrence's critique of "Bismarckianism," a version of "state-supervised capitalism" conducted by "a united German people."[21] In *D. H. Lawrence and Germany*, Carl Krockel examines the influence of German culture before and after the war on Lawrence's writing. Pointing out the realism of *Women in Love*, Krockel claims that Lawrence expresses the "social and economic alienation on the continent" and "uses

---

[21] James Scott, "'Continental': The Germanic Dimension of *Women in Love*," *Literatur in Wissenschaft und Unterricht* 12 (1979): 120.

the mining industry as an emblem of social, economic and political modernization."[22] In Krockel's view, Worthen and other critics who consider Lawrence's treatment of mining to be "more concerned with myth than with history" fail to recognize the significance of his references to Germany (161).

In 1916—or any year thereafter—references to German culture in an English text had political significance. In *English Modernism, National Identity and the Germans, 1890–1950*, Petra Rau surveys the frequent use of Germany as a trope in English fiction. Her study suggests that Lawrence's many references to Germany in *Women in Love* were characteristic of the period.[23] For example, Gerald "refused to go to Oxford, choosing a German university."[24] Birkin asks Gerald to swear a *Blutbrüderschaft* in imitation of "the old German knights" (206). Winifred's ferocious rabbit is named Bismarck, a creature described in the languages of three combatant nations: "'Bismarck is a mystery, Bismarck, c'est un mystère, der Bismarck, er ist ein Wunder,' said Gudrun, in mocking incantation" (237). Gudrun fantasizes that Gerald, with her support, could surpass Bismarck: "And Gerald would be freer, more dauntless than Bismarck" (418). Rau amplifies the political implications of allusions like these by showing that they were common in British national discourse.

In addition to explicit references to Germany, the theme of aggression has an immediate connection to the war. Parallels between sexual and social hostility in the novel are not so much a diagnosis

---

[22] Carl Krockel, *D. H. Lawrence and Germany: The Politics of Influence* (Amsterdam-New York, NY: Rodopi, 2007), 162.

[23] Petra Rau, *English Modernism, National Identity and the Germans, 1890–1950* (Surrey: Ashgate Publishing, 2009), 1–2.

[24] Lawrence, *Women in Love*, 221.

that one is the cause of the other as evidence that conflict is pervasive. The unexpected, even shocking, manifestation of women's murderous rage at their lovers suggests that violence is more fundamental and more widespread than organized military action. The images of Hermione striking Birkin at Breadalby and Gudrun striking Gerald in the Tyrol stretch the scene of violence across Europe. Smashing Birkin's head with a lapis sphere, Hermione feels purified by having performed an authentic act: "She was going to have her consummation of voluptuous ecstasy at last.... Then swiftly... she brought down the ball of jewel stone with all her force, crash on his head" (105). Gudrun repeats Hermione's gesture: "She raised her clenched hand high, and brought it down, with a great downward stroke, over the face and on to the breast of Gerald" (471). Giving these attacks the spiritual and sexual valence of a "consummation," Lawrence suggests the allure of war. The women's assaults release pent-up emotions that differ in their particulars but are similar in their aim of dominating the other, even if it means destroying him.

The novel explores the pervasive quest for dominance in a variety of cases, both human and animal. Gerald subjugates his mare and Winifred's rabbit, as well as the miners. Loerke beats his model into submission for the sake of his art. When Birkin's cat hits a female stray, the feline struggle introduces a discussion of the roots of violence in a specifically German context. Ursula quotes Nietzsche as she compares the cat's behavior to Gerald's abuse of his horse: "It is just like Gerald Crich with his horse—a lust for bullying—a real Wille zur Macht—so base, so petty" (150). Lawrence also alludes to the dialectic of power in Hegel's master-slave parable. Ursula wants a declaration of love, but Birkin objects: "'Proud and subservient, proud and subservient, I know you,' he retorted dryly. 'Proud and subserved, then subservient to the proud—I know you and your love. It is a tick-tack, tick-tack, a dance of opposites'" (153). The "tick-tack" dynamic recurs when Gudrun imagines living with Gerald at Shortlands: "The terrible bondage of this tick-tack of time, this twitching of the hands of the clock, this eternal repetition of hours and days,—Oh God, it was too awful to contemplate. And there was no escape from it, no escape" (464). Her life would be a "terrible bondage" because she would be subject to Gerald's will. The use of "tick-tack" as the "dance of opposites" and as the sound of time connects the two scenes. Allusions to German philosophers in these scenes expand the symbolic significance of the lovers' conflicts.

Personal and political relationships pivot on the word "will." Lawrence connects Nietzsche's *Wille zur Macht* to Kaiser Wilhelm II's troubling lament for the dead after the first year of the war: "*Vor Gott und der Geschichte ist mein Gewissen rein. Ich habe den Krieg nicht gewollt* ... Before God and history my conscience is clear. I did not will the war."[25] In the *First 'Women in Love'* Birkin echoes these words as he absolves himself in advance of any pain Ursula might feel in the future: "And if we go wrong—I shall know—ich habe es nicht gewollt."[26] In the 1921 text, however, Birkin utters the Kaiser's words after Gerald's death, crying, "I didn't want it to be like this—I didn't want it to be like this," and Lawrence makes the reference explicit: "Ursula could but think of the Kaiser's: 'Ich habe es nicht gewollt.' She looked almost with horror on Birkin."[27] Although the

---

[25] Lawrence, *Women in Love*, 585, note to 479.39.
[26] Lawrence, *First 'Women in Love,'* 294.
[27] Lawrence, *Women in Love*, 479.

Kaiser exonerates himself, he cannot mitigate the effects of aggressive policies. The echo links Gerald to the soldiers whose lives ended in pointless battle and implies that Birkin's remorse is as futile as the Kaiser's. This use of "will" to deny responsibility is the opposite of Nietzsche's "will to power," dramatizing the disparity between intentions and consequences.

The symbolic meanings of the text are not all negative. An image of creative harmony counters the violent pursuit of power. In a scene unchanged from the 1916 text, Lawrence boldly portrays German and English guests vacationing together in a Tyrolean inn, though the Tyrol was a brutal battlefront from 1915 to 1916. While the scene is a set piece that establishes the realistic setting, uncanny elements generate symbolic possibilities as well. The host at the inn presents the English guests to the Germans already gathered in the Reunionsaal. Loerke is telling a joke, a "recitation in the Cologne dialect" (405). The host interrupts him to introduce the newcomers, and then Loerke resumes his performance. Although their understanding of German is imperfect, the English guests begin to laugh too:

> The Germans were doubled up with laughter, hearing his strange, droll words, his droll phrases of dialect. And in the midst of their paroxysms, they glanced with deference at the four English strangers, the elect. Gudrun and Ursula were forced to laugh. Then the room rang with shouts of laughter .... Ursula looked round amazed, the laughter was bubbling out of her involuntarily. She looked at Gudrun, Gudrun looked at her: and the two sisters burst out laughing, carried away. Loerke glanced at them swiftly, with his full eyes. Birkin was sniggering involuntarily, Gerald Crich

sat erect, with a glistening look of amusement on his face. And the laugher crashed out again, in wild paroxysms, the Professor's daughters were reduced to shaking helplessness, the veins in the Professor's neck were swollen, his face was purple, he was strangled in ultimate silent spasms of laughter, the students were shouting half-articulated words that tailed off in helpless explosions. (406)

Extremity and rhetorical exaggeration add symbolic meanings to the realistic situation. Words like "paroxysms," "strangled," "crashed," and "explosions" undermine the common assumption that laughter is a sign of happiness. The passage suggests that both violence and laughter have unconscious sources and involve being "carried away" and acting "involuntarily." The guests are "forced to laugh," reduced to "helplessness." The image of the professor "strangled" with laughter invites comparison with a later scene when Gerald, overcome by murderous rage, tries to strangle Gudrun. In both situations there is a loss of self-consciousness and self-control. If, as Freud argues, aggression is the source of violence as well as humor, manifestations of aggression range from assaults to jokes.[28]

Just as "paroxysms" have antithetical causes, language differences have antithetical consequences. Nationalist aspirations based on native languages were one of the factors leading to war, but in this scene dialects lead to general laughter. After listening to Loerke's

---

[28] Sigmund Freud, *Jokes and Their Relation to the Unconscious (1905)*, Standard Edition of the Complete Psychological Works of Sigmund Freud, vol. 8, trans. and ed. James Strachey (London: Hogarth Press, 1960), 96–97. Freud argues that jokes are a social expression of unconscious wishes, just as dreams are an individual expression of the same wishes. He claims that jokes either express hostility, "serving the purpose of aggressiveness, satire, or defence," or obscenity, "serving the purpose of exposure."

story, Ursula says, "And we couldn't understand it."[29] Nevertheless, the four English guests join in the hilarity. Their laughter is inexplicable, yet it dissolves antagonism and unites the strangers: "The mixture was made, the new-comers were stirred into the party, like new ingredients, the whole room was alive" (406). The group's laughter is not joyous, but it marks the absence of will. Whereas an individual's thwarted drive for dominance leads to rage and violence, being able to yield to another leads to laughter. In contrast to adversaries seeking power over each other, the guests form a community through humor.

In the spirit of communal feeling, Ursula sings "Annie Laurie." The refrain of the ballad "And for bonnie Annie Laurie/I'd lay me doon and dee" makes death a symbol of the depth and constancy of the lover's feelings. The metaphor of dying for love in the song has a literal parallel in the patriotic sacrifice of soldiers. Ursula's performance transcends the meaning of the lyrics. Flattered by the attention of the German guests, she emerges from Birkin's shadow: "Birkin was well in the background, ... she was liberated into overweening self-confidence" (407). Her singing transforms her and her audience: "She was as happy as the sun that has just opened above clouds. And everybody seemed so admiring and radiant, it was perfect" (407). She feels fulfilled and makes others feel "radiant" as well. As the German guests say, she is truly an artist: "die gnädige Frau ist wirklich eine Künstlerin, aber wirklich!" (407). Ursula is neither dominated nor submissive, and her happiness as she performs a song about love and death is the opposite of the will to power.

---

[29] Lawrence, *Women in Love*, 406.

Lawrence enhances the symbolic significance of this extraordinary moment by portraying Loerke as a magical figure, sinister and gifted with special powers. He is an "odd creature, like a child, and like a troll, quick, detached" (405). Everything about him is mismatched. He is the "little man with the boyish figure, and the round, full, sensitive-looking head, and the quick, full eyes, like a mouse's" (405), and his "body was slight and unformed, like a boy's, but his voice was mature, sardonic, its movement had the flexibility of essential energy, and of a mocking, penetrating understanding" (406). Petra Rau claims that Loerke's "overdetermined hybridity" is a "representation of the grotesque as a 'confusion.'"[30] In its extremity, this confusion extends the range of Loerke's symbolic meanings.

Although Loerke is usually considered the embodiment of everything Lawrence despised, there are also similarities between them. As Brenda Maddox notes, Lawrence's family thought of him as "the runt of the litter," and he was a "wicked mimic."[31] A more substantive resemblance is that Loerke is a professional artist. He supports himself by selling his sculpture. Unlike Lawrence, however, Loerke regards artists as workers. He believes that life is "nothing but work" and that work is the proper subject of art: "Art should *interpret* industry, as art once interpreted religion."[32] Rau notes that this aesthetic was also promulgated by the *Werkbund*, another alliance of artists in prewar Germany.[33] Founded in 1907, the *Werkbund* was devoted to reconciling art and industry. As the

---

[30] Rau, *English Modernism*, 146.
[31] Brenda Maddox, *D. H. Lawrence: The Story of a Marriage* (New York: Simon & Schuster, 1994), 38 and 27.
[32] Lawrence, *Women in Love*, 424.
[33] Rau, *English Modernism*, 143.

art historian Frederic J. Schwartz observes, the *Werkbund* advocated "artists' designs based on new formal principles that would both express and take into account modern conditions of production and use, modern objects and materials, in short modernity in general."[34] A secondary goal was to involve artists in designing everyday objects for a mass market (9). These goals are implicit in Loerke's pronouncements, and they reappear in Post-Expressionists' images of everyday things.

Loerke advocates other aesthetic principles when convenient. To conceal the personal meaning of his sculpture, he invokes formalism. He insists that his statuette of a young girl on a stallion "is a work of art, it is a picture of nothing, of absolutely nothing."[35] Ursula, however, accurately perceives the lived experience that led to the piece: "The horse is a picture of your own stock stupid brutality, and the girl was a girl you loved and tortured and then ignored" (431). Loerke later validates Ursula's insight, admitting, "She was a nuisance—not for a minute would she keep still—not until I'd slapped her hard and made her cry—then she'd sit for five minutes" (433). His willingness to use violence to produce his work discredits his claim that art has nothing to do with life. Ursula parries his formalism with a more traditional aesthetic principle, proclaiming, "The world of art is only the truth about the real world, that's all—but you are too far gone to see it" (431). Gudrun and Loerke consider Ursula's conviction naïve, but it echoes what Lawrence says in his 1919 Foreword: "This novel pretends only to be a record of the writer's own desire, aspirations,

---

[34] Frederic J. Schwartz, *The Werkbund: Design Theory and Mass Culture before the First World War* (New Haven and London: Yale University Press, 1996), 9.
[35] Lawrence, *Women in Love*, 430.

struggles: in a word, a record of the profoundest experiences in the self" (485). In the novel, however, each aesthetic position is qualified by its narrative context. It is the sentimental Germans who say that Ursula is the real artist.

Writing at the height of the war, Lawrence imagined a microcosm of English and German guests in a mountain inn. They laugh and sing and dance together. These are not transcendent acts. They involve mockery, flirtation, and jealousy, but they are not violent. Being subject to another's will causes rage and violence; listening to a joke leads to communal laughter. Although it is possible to read the novel as an escape from contemporary events, the characters' personal encounters suggest political parallels. The alternative to the will to power is the willingness to accept another's autonomy, and these options play out in various combinations.

The war could not be ignored. It caused Lawrence and many others who believed that immaterial experience was the essence of life to reconsider the significance of material circumstances. In June 1914, Lawrence had described *The Rainbow* in Expressionist terms. His subject would no longer be the particular individual but the constants of human behavior. Comparing individual differences to the "allotropic states" of an element, he wrote his editor, "The ordinary novel would trace the history of the diamond—but I say 'diamond, what! This is carbon.' And my diamond might be coal or soot, and my theme is carbon."[36] By 1916, however, the difference between diamond and coal mattered. *Women in Love* encompasses

---

[36] Lawrence, *Letters*, vol. 2, 183.

public and private life, economic and aesthetic theories, empirical and nonempirical experience. Having adopted the Expressionists' use of abstraction to represent subjectivity, Lawrence was able to see its limits. He did not repudiate symbolism, but he gave it a realistic foundation. Whether this combination was called Post-Expressionism or modernism, it was not an escape from social issues but an avant-garde response to the war.

4

Ulysses, the mythical method, and magic realism

It is impossible to exaggerate the importance of *Ulysses*. Formally, it is the definitive modernist text—original, difficult, allusive, ironic. Thematically, it examines the vicissitudes of personal and political commitments—marriage, religion, nationalism. Like Lawrence, Joyce avoided direct references to the war being fought as he wrote. His story takes place on a day in Dublin in 1904, long before the Easter Uprising or Verdun, but the book is named for a warrior returning from Troy. Joyce portrays a complex world that contains the seeds of public violence—as well as everything else—and he addresses the persistent question of how to represent violence in a secular age. If, as Stephen Dedalus remarks, history is a nightmare, is it to be represented as fact or fantasy? Joyce's answer is that extremity, excess, and irony make the meaning of narratives about contemporary life indeterminate, demonstrating how to respond to recent events without explaining, justifying, or condemning them.

T. S. Eliot was one of the first to interpret *Ulysses* in relation to the current social crisis. Although Joyce does not portray the Irish

Rebellion or the First World War directly, in his 1923 essay "*Ulysses,* Order, and Myth" Eliot hails the book as a breakthrough in solving the artistic problem of dealing with "the immense panorama of futility and anarchy which is contemporary history."[1] Eliot calls *Ulysses* "the most important expression which the present age has found; it is a book to which we are all indebted, and from which none of us can escape" (175). He credits Joyce with nothing less than "making the modern world possible for art" (178).[2]

While Charles Taylor calls attention to the fragilization of beliefs in a secular culture, Eliot sees only futility and anarchy. In such a world, there is no logic of cause and effect to connect actions to consequences, and narrative is untenable. Accordingly, Eliot pronounces the death of the novel: "The novel ended with Flaubert and with James" (177). He declares: "Instead of narrative method, we may now use the mythical method" (178). He credits Joyce and W. B. Yeats with the discovery that "in manipulating a continuous parallel between contemporaneity and antiquity" (177), they could themselves construct "order and form" (178). Joyce's use of the *Odyssey* is "simply a way of controlling, of ordering, of giving a shape and a significance" to modern life (177). Although the acts of "controlling" and "ordering" have acquired the negative associations of political control and repressive order, they are fundamental to the aims of

---

[1] Eliot, "*Ulysses,* Order, and Myth," 177.
[2] Other readings of *Ulysses* as a response to the First World War and violence in Ireland include Robert Spoo, "'Nestor' and the Nightmare: The Presence of the Great War in *Ulysses,*" in *Joyce and the Subject of History,* ed. Mark A. Wolleager, Victor Luftig, and Robert Spoo (Ann Arbor: University of Michigan Press, 1996); Emer Nolan, *James Joyce and Nationalism* (London and New York: Routledge, 1995); Enda Duffy, *The Subaltern "Ulysses"* (Minneapolis and London: University of Minnesota Press, 1994).

finding "shape" and "significance," aims that later writers reiterated. The mythical method, Eliot claims, is like a scientific discovery that alters a field for all future practitioners. He predicts, "Mr. Joyce is pursuing a method which others must pursue after him" (177), and they did.

Although Eliot speaks of a single "continuous parallel between contemporaneity and antiquity," Joyce uses multiple parallels. While Eliot mentions Joyce's use of the *Odyssey*, *Ulysses* coordinates its account of a day in Dublin with innumerable systems. Each episode is assigned an hour, an organ of the body, a color, a symbol, an art, and a "Technic,"[3] and there are recurring references to icons of high and low culture as various as *Hamlet*, the Wandering Jew, and *Venus in Furs*. Eliot recommends a comparable range of sources for others who might employ the mythical method: "It is a method for which the horoscope is auspicious. Psychology (such as it is, and whether our reaction to it be comic or serious), ethnology, and *The Golden Bough* have concurred to make possible what was impossible even a few years ago."[4] This eclectic array, stretching from the occult to social science, from historical to imagined antecedents, suggests that Eliot welcomed patterns wherever they might be found. He is not recommending these systems because of their beliefs but because they offer patterns that can be applied to contemporary events. While Joyce's parallels to the *Odyssey* invoke traditional myths, other parallels do not. As Eliot's diverse list suggests, in the absence of any consensus about the foundation of meaning, only the structure of

---

[3] Stuart Gilbert, *James Joyce's "Ulysses": A Study* (New York: Vintage, 1952), 29.
[4] Eliot, "*Ulysses*, Order, and Myth," 177–78.

meaning can be affirmed. A more accurate title for the essay might be "*Ulysses*, Orders, and Myths."

Nevertheless, many critics assume that the mythical method imposes fixed meanings on contemporary events.[5] For example, Fredric Jameson objects that the idea of myth gives *Ulysses* and other texts a false unity:

> As for the mythical interpretation—the Odyssey parallel undoubtedly underscored for us by the text itself as well as by generations of slavish interpreters—here too it would be desirable to think of something else. We are today, one would hope, well beyond that moment of classical modernism and its ideologies in which, as Sartre said somewhere, there was a "myth of myth," in which the very notion of some mythic unity and reconciliation was used in a mythical, or as I would prefer to say, a fetishised way. The bankruptcy of the ideology of the mythic is only one feature of the bankruptcy of the ideology of modernism in general; yet it

---

[5] See Kevin J. H. Dettmar, *The Illicit Joyce of Postmodernism: Reading against the Grain* (Madison: University of Wisconsin Press, 1996), 162–65. Dettmar summarizes critical interpretations of the Homeric parallels in *Ulysses*. See also Spoo, "'Nestor,'" 107, on the "convergence of history and story" in relation to Eliot's mythical method. Spoo concludes that "the variety and complexity of historical textures in *Ulysses*" makes Eliot's concept harder to accept: "Such a method would require a static conception of history in which present and past are distinct from one another and observable by an ordering consciousness" (120). Yet Spoo's description of *Ulysses* is consistent with my understanding of the mythical method: "*Ulysses* is committed to symbolically intensive rather than temporally extensive revelations of plot and character, and it relies upon symbol and theme to gesture toward potentialities when character development is forced to recede. The narrative present therefore becomes saturated with the past and the future, in some cases overdetermined by them, so that the present naturalistic moment is never quite itself and cannot be taken at face value. Stephen's students are both hockey players and infantrymen, schoolboys and victims" (113–14).

is a most interesting one, on which (had we more time) it might have been instructive to dwell.[6]

Jameson's reading stalls at a fixed idea of myth, never reaching Eliot's point about method. Although Eliot discusses the parallel between *Ulysses* and the *Odyssey*, he minimizes the importance of classical allusions. He disagrees with those who claim that the Homeric parallels in *Ulysses* are "an amusing dodge, or scaffolding erected by the author for the purpose of disposing his realistic tale."[7] Eliot conceives of the mythical method as a structural principle rather than as an infusion of meaning from the past into the present. Parallels between seemingly unique events of the moment and historical or imagined antecedents, such as the correspondence between Bloom and Odysseus, create meaningful patterns. His essay defines the mythical method as a strategy for constructing a relationship between contemporary life and something else—in fact, anything else.

By aligning the anarchy and futility of the present with something else, the mythical method makes chaotic events parts of meaningful patterns. The multiplicity of incompatible patterns keeps each of them contingent. In the absence of a social consensus about the relationship between cause and effect, past and present, and acts and consequences, the mythical method constructs arbitrary relationships. It is a structure, not a set of beliefs. Far from being an authoritarian quest for stasis and order, the mythical method maintains the structure of meaning without affirming a particular

---

[6] Jameson, "*Ulysses* in History," 146.
[7] Eliot "*Ulysses*, Order, and Myth," 175.

meaning. The crucial difference between the mythical method and myths is its multiplicity.

Eliot's explanation of *Ulysses* as a response to "the immense panorama of futility and anarchy which is contemporary history" has become so familiar that it barely conveys the urgency artists felt at the time. It may now sound arch and mannered, but in the 1920s Eliot was groping for a lifeline rather than laying down the law. Eliot claims that Joyce's general method—not only the obvious parallel to the *Odyssey* but also "the use of appropriate styles and symbols to each division" (175)—is Joyce's most significant achievement. Summarizing the initial critical reaction to *Ulysses*, Derek Attridge notes that whereas Joyce's detractors objected to the formal difficulty of the text, most of his early supporters minimized the significance of the innovative style. Instead, they focused on "the vividness of psychological detail and the concreteness of the setting ... to turn the book into a super-realist novel; by stressing the structural ingenuity of the book as a rewriting of the *Odyssey* one could reassure readers that it was not the chaotic mess it seemed at first."[8] In contrast, Attridge argues that *Ulysses* is a central modernist text largely because of its "*excess* of technique," which is "not designed to thwart meaning, but to multiply meanings" (154). Eliot was one of the first to make this point. Unlike most of the book's early admirers, he believed that Joyce's style was his great breakthrough.

The absence of any stable or authoritative parallel "between contemporanaeity and antiquity" makes the mythical method

---

[8] Derek Attridge, "Joyce and the Making of Modernism: The Question of Technique," in *Rethinking Modernism*, ed. Marianne Thormählen (New York: Palgrave Macmillan, 2003), 156.

fundamentally ironic. It is not the verbal irony of saying one thing and meaning another, or the dramatic irony of the audience knowing more than the characters do, or the Swiftian irony of a speaker who is indifferent to the ethical implications of his statements. *Ulysses* introduces a radical narrative irony that does not depend on a speaker's intentions. Instead, the range of scenes and social discourses in the text prevents readers from discerning any consistent narrative tone or point of view. The disparity between scenes and narrative voices (rather than between what a speaker says and means) produces pervasive irony. Since style conforms to the habits and assumptions embedded in conventions of discourse, it no longer reinforces character, action, or mood.

Eliot's account of the mythical method resembles Franz Roh's analysis of postwar German art in his 1925 book *Nach-Expressionismus: Magischer Realismus* (Post-Expressionism: Magic Realism).[9] This is the same movement that Gustav Hartlaub called "Neue Sachlichkeit" (New Objectivity) when he organized an exhibit of postwar art in 1923, and art historians prefer his term.[10] Wieland

---

[9] Franz Roh, *Nach-Expressionismus: Magischer Realismus* (Leipzig: Klinkhardt & Biermann, 1925). I provide the original German text because the book is not widely available, nor has it been translated into English in its entirety. Selections were published in Spanish as "Realismo mágico: Problemas de la pintura europea más reciente" in *Revista de Occidente* 16 (1927): 274–301. Wendy B. Faris translated this version and published it as "Magic Realism: Post-Expressionism (1925)" in *Magical Realism: Theory, History, Community*, ed. Lois Parkinson Zamora and Wendy B. Faris (Durham and London: Duke University Press, 1995), 15–31. I cite her translation as "Faris" and the German source as "Roh" with respective page numbers. Translations of Roh that are not credited are my own.

[10] On the ambiguity of the term "magic realism" since the 1920s, see Irene Guenther, "Magic Realism, New Objectivity, and the Arts during the Weimar Republic" in *Magical Realism: Theory, History, Community*, ed. Lois Parkinson Zamora and Wendy B. Faris (Durham and London: Duke University Press, 1995), 33–73. Guenther argues that the emigration of German-speaking artists, critics, and historians to Central and South America eventually

Schmied affirms, "Both German phrases, 'Neue Sachlichkeit' and 'Magischer Realismus', then denoted one and the same thing; the difference was only one of emphasis. Both referred to a mode of representation which had come into being 'after the disappearance of the expressionist manner', and which was 'firm in compositional structure but once more representational' ... and both terms were intended to have an application that went beyond contemporary German art."[11] In 1927, W. E. Süskind (whose son Patrick published the magic realist novel *Perfume: The Story of a Murderer* in 1986) noted that "Neue Sachlichkeit" had become "a catchphrase," *ein Schlagwort*, for postwar art of all kinds.[12]

Roh's oxymoron, however, captures the duality of the art itself; the new movement supplements the spiritual aims of Expressionism with the empirical references of realism. Roh defines magic realism as an attempt to locate meaning in a specific time and place, and the same could be said about *Ulysses*.[13] He explains that in contrast to the

led to Alejo Carpentier's appropriation of the term for postcolonial writing in 1949. Guenther also traces the influence of magic realist painting on German writers such as Carl Sternheim, Heinrich Mann, George Kaiser, Bertholt Brecht, and Walter Mehring. For a more recent summary of competing definitions of magic realism, see Christopher Warnes, "The Hermeneutics of Vagueness: Magical Realism in Current Literary Critical Discourse," *Journal of Postcolonial Writing* 41 (2005): 1–13. Warnes establishes the maturity of the genre when he notes that in May 2002 *Newsweek International* asked, "Is Magical Realism Dead?" (1). For another survey of definitions of magic realism, see Michael Valdes Moses, "Magical Realism at World's End," *Literary Imagination: The Review of the Association of Literary Scholars and Critics* 3 (2001): 108, n. 5.

[11] Wieland Schmied, "Neue Sachlichkeit and German Realism of the Twenties," in *German Realism of the Twenties: The Artist as Social Critic*, ed. Louise Lincoln (Minneapolis: Minneapolis Institute of Arts, 1980), 42.

[12] Peter de Mendelssohn, *S. Fischer und sein Verlag* (Frankfurt am Main: S. Fischer Verlag, 1970), 1091.

[13] See John Gordon, *Joyce and Reality: The Empirical Strikes Back* (Syracuse, NY: Syracuse University Press, 2004), xiii–xiv. Gordon points out that the blend of realist fiction and Symbolist poetry in *Ulysses* is widely recognized: "As Harry Levin pointed out long ago,

abstract spirituality of Expressionism, postwar artists represent the "magic of being" while also recognizing that "things already have their own faces."[14] Post-Expressionist paintings are not realistic, but they are far more concrete than Expressionist images.

Roh claims that magic realism locates meaning in the material world by sustaining a tension between "the forms of the spirit and the very solidity of objects" (22).[15] He carefully defines "spirit" in secular terms: "The point is not to discover the spirit beginning with objects but, on the contrary, to discover objects beginning with the spirit" (24).[16] In a religious culture, artists can assume the immanence of the divine in the created world and attempt to "discover the spirit beginning with objects." Postwar artists, however, reverse the process. They seek the object that will express their meaning: they "discover objects beginning with the spirit." Roh adds, "With the word 'magic,' as opposed to 'mystic,' I wish to indicate that the mystery does not descend to the represented world, but rather hides and palpitates behind it" (16).[17] "Mystic" implies a supernatural presence, but magic is a human trick. Magic realism locates nonempirical meaning in empirical reality without claiming a divine foundation.

in his aesthetic program Joyce positioned himself between the twin inheritances of late-nineteenth-century naturalism and late-nineteenth-century *symbolisme*—Zola and Mallarmé, objective truth and subjective truth—and looked for guidance to those writers, especially Flaubert and Ibsen, whom he believed had brought the two together with some success." See also Franz Roh, *Nach-Expressionismus*, 110. Roh, however, credits Zola and Rimbaud rather than Mallarmé as the representative Symbolist poet.

[14] Faris, "Magic Realism," 20.

[15] Roh writes: "Aber auch hier werden die Gefüge des Geistigen in harte Spannung gesetzt mit der Eigenfestigkeit der Objekte ..." (34).

[16] Roh writes: "Es wird also nicht von den Objekten zum Geist gefunden, sondern von diesem zu den Objekten ..." (37).

[17] Roh writes: "Mit 'magisch' im Gegensatz zu 'mystisch' sollte angedeutet sein, daß das Geheimnis nicht in die dargestellte Welt eingeht, sondern sich hinter ihr zurückhält (was sich im Verlauf erklären mag)" (n.p.).

Although words like "spirit" and "mystery" suggest religion and the occult, Roh points out that in the new art political and social ideas have replaced revelation: "The religious and transcendental themes have largely disappeared in recent painting. In contrast, we are offered a new style that is thoroughly of this world, that celebrates the mundane" (17).[18] Emphasizing the secular basis of this art, Roh stipulates that "spirit" does not imply religious belief. He formulates the difference in an aphorism: "Instead of the remote horrors of hell, the inextinguishable horrors of our own time" (17).[19] Neither transcending nor ignoring material reality, postwar art conveys symbolic meanings but limits them by referring to a particular time and place.

Defining magic realism as a reaction against Expressionism, Roh lists a number of differences between the two movements. In contrast to the many religious themes of Expressionism, magic realism is secular.[20] Magic realism attaches meaning to particulars rather than abstractions. The abstract forms of Expressionism create an effect of "summary" that Roh contrasts with the "thoroughness" and specificity of magic realist painting.[21] Unlike the "monumentality" of Expressionism, magic realism focuses on the "miniature" (119).[22] The microscopic perspective produces an excess of detail that "establishes

---

[18] Roh writes: "Die religiöse oder transzendente Thematik ist meist geschwunden: ein Hauptzug dieser neuen Malerei. Dafür ist eine innig irdische, eine weltfromme Art hervorgetreten" (24).

[19] Roh writes: "Statt entlegener Höllengreuel die unausgerotteten Greuel unserer eigenen Zeit (Gross, Dix)" (24).

[20] Roh, Nach-Expressionismus, 119. Roh lists "Viel religiöse Vorwürfe" under Expressionism and "Sehr wenig religiöse Vorwürfe" under Post-Expressionism. This dichotomy does not appear in Irene Guenther's translation of Roh's 1958 "Schema" in "Magic Realism," 35–36.

[21] Roh's terms are "Summarisch" and "Durchfürend."

[22] Roh's terms are "Monumental" and "Miniaturartig."

the largest possible number of subdivisions."[23] The proliferation of details, however, is symbolic because the miniaturist attempts "to locate *infinity* in small things" (27).[24] Emphasizing the integrative thrust of the new art, Roh characterizes the artistic energy of magic realism as a "centripetal" rather than a "centrifugal" force.[25]

To illustrate the change, Roh also presents pairs of paintings, such as Kandinsky's *Reiter* (Figure 4.1) and Carlo Carrà's *Reiter* (Figure 4.2).[26] Whereas Kandinsky uses a few lines to suggest the essence of horse and rider in motion, Carrà's image contains far more information. There is a building; there is ground; horse and rider bear armor. These cultural references specify the context for interpretation. Recalibrating the balance between realism and abstraction, postwar art represents identifiable people, places, and things, yet everything is distorted. The images are concrete but not mimetic. This style is not a return to realism, but an attempt to anchor meanings in the material world.

The new art is specific about people, places, and things but not about meaning. "Object" and "spirit" are Roh's terms for the components of the aesthetic mixture that Eliot calls "history" and "myth." Neither Eliot's "mythical method" nor Roh's "magic realism" implies belief in the supernatural. Both terms refer to art that proposes secular rather than religious meanings for contemporary events. Approaching the new art from different

---

[23] Faris, "Magic Realism," 28. Roh writes: "Weiter führt schon die Erkenntnis, daß der monumentalisierende Mensch alles zu großen Blöken ballt, während der mikroskopierende möglichst viel Unterteilungen setzt" (58).

[24] Roh writes: "die aus einer Gesinnung hervorgeht, die die Unendlichkeit des Kleinen sucht" (57).

[25] Guenther, "Magic Realism," 36. This binary does not appear in Roh's 1925 "Schema."

[26] The illustrations appear in Roh, *Nach-Expressionismus: Magischer Realismus*, n.p.

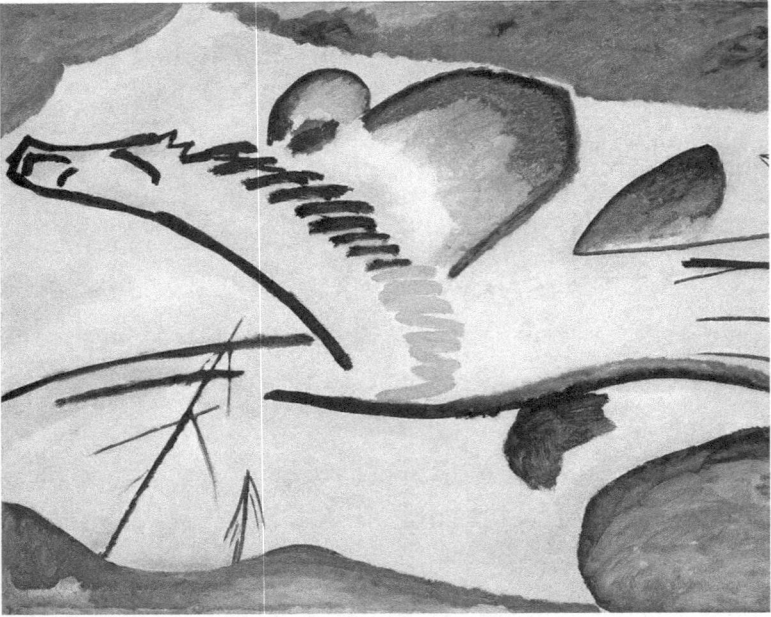

FIGURE 4.1 *Wassily Kandinsky,* **Reiter** *(1912).*

FIGURE 4.2 *Carlo Carrà,* **Reiter** *(1917).*

directions, however, Eliot notices its symbolism, whereas Roh emphasizes its objectivity. From Eliot's perspective, Joyce's symbolism and stylistic innovations stand out against the strong realist tradition in English fiction. From Roh's perspective, postwar art seems objective in relation to the abstraction and subjectivism of Expressionism. Having seen that spiritual energy was a volatile force that could be invoked to justify antithetical ends, German artists were disillusioned with the vague idealism of Expressionism. They wanted to connect nonempirical meanings and empirical experience. This combination, rather than an alternative spiritual reality, was the basis of the new art.

The contrast between Eliot and Roh illustrates Modris Eksteins's generalization about the differences between England and Germany before the war. Whereas England had a strong empirical tradition, Eksteins argues, Germany was susceptible to appeals for mythic unity: "Germany's essential ethos, then, before 1914, involved a search for new forms, forms conceived not in terms of laws and finiteness but in terms of symbol, metaphor, and myth."[27] After the war, artists who held antithetical political convictions nevertheless agreed that Expressionism was too vague and malleable. Many who had been Expressionists before the war joined the new movement. As Peter Selz notes, "In 1912 the German art historian and critic Wilhelm Hausenstein, a strong advocate of expressionism at the time, concurred with the move toward abstraction, declaring that 'art which is tied to the object is a primitive form of art.' But eight years later, after the end of the war, Hausenstein reversed his position and welcomed

---

[27] Eksteins, *Rites of Spring*, 81.

the 'salvation of the individual in the object.'"[28] The war discredited the Expressionist solution to the problem of representing secularity.

In the absence of a consensus of belief, the relationship between empirical reality and meaning had to be constructed. Magic realist artists tried to tie immaterial meanings to the particulars of material experience. Lacking the stability of religious belief, the links between objects and meanings were contingent, variable, and indeterminate. To create these unstable bonds, artists animated objects and objectified animate beings. Something askew indicated that recognizable objects were to be interpreted as symbols with multiple meanings.

Despite the diversity of subject matter and technique in magic realist paintings, the unifying factor of the new art was its conviction that every idea had to be grounded in material reality. Nevertheless, many of the paintings that Roh cites as examples of the new art are less objective than he implies. They represent recognizable people, places, and objects but depart from realism to give ordinary things an extraordinary significance. Artists such as Otto Dix, George Grosz, Alexander Kanoldt, Christian Schaad, and George Schrimpf differ greatly, but they all introduce something at odds with objective reality to make their paintings seem eerie, uncanny, or ironic. Although these paintings do not portray the fantastic events of later magic realist fiction, some of them could be used to illustrate it. For example, the grotesque faces of a boy and a girl in Dix's *Zwei Kinder* (1921) (Figure 4.3) suggest the street children in *The Tin Drum*. Schrimpf's *Auf der Treppe/Am*

---

[28] Peter Selz, "Artist as Social Critic," in *German Realism of the Twenties: The Artist as Social Critic*, ed. Louise Lincoln (Minneapolis: Minneapolis Institute of Arts, 1980), 29.

FIGURE 4.3 *Otto Dix,* **Zwei Kinder** *(1921).*

Abend (1924) (Figure 4.4) evokes the timelessness, immobility, and isolation of *One Hundred Years of Solitude*.

The political spectrum of Roh's visual examples extends from the socialism of George Grosz on the left to the nationalism of George Schrimpf on the right. Roh accounts for this range in aesthetic terms,

FIGURE 4.4 *George Schrimpf,* **Auf der Treppe/Am Abend** *(1924–25).*

saying that "the most recent art corresponds ... to a third class of man":
"This kind of man is neither the 'empirical' Machiavellian politician
nor the apolitical man who listens only to the voice of an ethical ideal,
but a man at once political *and* ethical, in whom both characteristics
are equally prominent."[29] Although Roh interprets the new art as a

---

[29] Faris, "Magic Realism," 23. Roh writes: "Dies ist weder der 'empirische Politiker' und
Macchiavellist, noch der unpolitische Nur-Ethiker, sondern der ethische homo politicus
mit gleichgewichtiger Betonung beider Begriffe" (35).

call to combine ideas and action, he does not specify what the ideas or acts must be. His point is that ethical principles and material reality should not be separated in life or in art. The structure he describes accommodates almost any content.

Roh's discussion of Dix and Grosz emphasizes the secular foundation of magic realism. Two similar paintings illustrate Roh's generalization about the artists' attention to the "horrors of our own time." Dix's *Selbstbildnis mit Modell* (1923) has been called his "Neue Sachlichkeit manifesto."[30] Dix portrays himself fully clothed standing next to a nude woman. His body is rigid, and he holds his arms straight at his sides, implying an effort of self-control. Ignoring the model, he stares angrily at something just beyond her. In contrast, the woman is all pliant curves. She is posed seductively with her arms raised, hands folded behind her head. She looks toward the viewer, submissively displaying her body. Although the woman is exposed in her nudity and wide-eyed gaze, neither figure acknowledges the presence of the other. The striking visual incongruity between the figures introduces a stylistic disparity comparable to the discordant discourses of *Ulysses*.

Grosz's *Mann und Frau* (1926) (Figure 4.5) also presents a fully clothed man and a nearly naked woman. The woman wears only a hat, a slip, and jewelry. Holding a hand mirror, she inspects her necklace as if it is a recent acquisition. A wall mirror on the right slants inward, compressing the picture space. Positioned between the wall mirror and her hand mirror, the woman is entirely self-absorbed. The man sits on the bed tying his shoe and casts a sidelong glance

---

[30] Ida Rigby, "Otto Dix, *Self-Portrait with Model*, 1923," in *German Realism of the Twenties: The Artist as Social Critic*, ed. Louise Lincoln (Minneapolis: Minneapolis Institute of Arts, 1980), 128.

FIGURE 4.5 *George Grosz,* **Mann und Frau** *(1926).*

at her body. One critic calls attention to the "calculating gaze and arrested motions" of the "leering man."[31] The cigarette in his mouth

---

[31] Beth Irwin Lewis, "George Grosz: *Man and Wife,* 1926," in *German Realism of the Twenties: The Artist as Social Critic,* ed. Louise Lincoln (Minneapolis: Minneapolis Institute of Arts, 1980), 127.

lines up with a corner of his shirt collar to form an arrow pointing to the woman's pubis. The woman's gaze, however, directs the viewer's attention to the value of the necklace rather than to her body. The composition suggests a circuit of desire passing from the man's erotic aim to the woman's economic aim. He scrutinizes her sexualized body, while she focuses on what he paid for it.

Like Dix, Grosz uses slightly different styles for each figure. The man is drawn like a caricature. A few distinct expression lines on his forehead, cheeks, and mouth convey his lust. The woman, however, is painted with the care typically given to the female nude. Her flesh is the visual focus of the painting. Painstaking technique produces the transparency of a slip that covers yet reveals her body. Her face is modeled with highlights and shadows rather than the thick, cartoonish lines of the man's face. Suggesting analogies to the many styles of *Ulysses*, Grosz's work has been described as a combination of "influences from various sources both from the world of high culture and from the mass media such as comic strips, the thriller, and serial novels."[32] Satirizing debased sexual relations, Grosz blends verisimilitude and distortion to launch his critique of contemporary life. Each figure and object is identifiable, evoking a specific time and place, yet the painting is not realistic. The lines are too wavy, the background is too sketchy, the colors are too blotchy, everything is too brown. The realistic elements convey the exchange of sex for "gifts" in postwar Germany. The distortion creates the tension between "object" and "spirit" that Roh identifies.

---

[32] Achille Bonito Oliva, "The Common Sense of the Grotesque," in *George Grosz: The Berlin Years*, ed. Serge Sabarsky (New York: Rizzoli International Publications, Inc., 1985), 17.

The inconsistent styles generate irony, leaving viewers and readers uncertain how respond.[33]

Although Roh's generalizations are based on paintings, he also discusses magic realism in literature.[34] He characterizes literary magic realism as a mixture of the symbolism of Rimbaud and the naturalism of Zola.[35] This early connection between postwar painting and literature has been obscured by art historians' preference for "Neue Sachlichkeit" (New Objectivity) over "magic realism." Since Roh focuses on the relation between cultural conditions and form, his discussion of magic realist painting highlights qualities that are also evident in *Ulysses* and its heirs. In magic realist fiction, as in *Ulysses*, extreme events generate symbolic meanings, and a superabundance of characters, information, allusions, and styles sustains myriad patterns. Secular excess replaces divine plenitude, and there is no authoritative voice or consistent tone to provide a hierarchy of significance. Digressions and extraneous details frustrate the reader's search for causes and explanations. Exaggerated correlations between public events and individual lives

---

[33] See Beth Irwin Lewis, "George Grosz," 127. Lewis reports that the models for the painting were Grosz's sister-in-law Lotte and her husband. A contemporary painting of Lotte alone, *Lotte in grünem Kleid* (89), in contrast, is executed in a single, consistent style and lacks the irony of *Mann und Frau*.

[34] Some critics object that since Roh's ideas were based on painting, they are irrelevant to literature. See, for example, Christopher Warnes, "The Hermeneutics of Vagueness," 8. Warnes writes: "Some definitions strive to encapsulate continuity between the term's uses in art-historical contexts and those that are more strictly literary in nature. An example of the kinds of distorting, and ultimately meaningless, comparisons that result from the application of overly general definitions can be found in an essay by Theo D'haen."

[35] Roh, 110. Roh writes: "Auch die literarische Wendung bringt gewisse Anfangs- und Endpunkte wieder näher zusammen: Die eine Welle ist mit neuer Schätzung A. Rimbauds verbunden. Neue veristische Neigungen aber haben neue Liebe zu Zola entstehen lassen." (The literary turn also brings certain beginning and end points close together again: one is a new esteem for Rimbaud. Yet new verist tendencies have let a new love for Zola arise.)

domesticate the former and aggrandize the latter. Terrible events are described comically, and everyday matters are treated as portents. These strategies destabilize every apparent statement of meaning. They preserve the structure of meaning without committing the text to any controlling meaning.

In Germany, *Ulysses* was considered a prime example of the new movement. Breon Mitchell reports, "Insofar as the novel was scientific and exact it seemed to reflect both the most recent developments of the age, and the particular stylistic tendencies of 'neue Sachlichkeit'. Joyce was characterized as the first author (in any language) to follow these tendencies to their logical conclusion."[36] Alfred Döblin's 1928 review of *Ulysses* emphasizes its resemblance to postwar art. Döblin interprets Joyce's text as a literary version of the specificity and range of meaning in magic realist painting. He agrees with Eliot's and Roh's analyses of the postwar aesthetic crisis and believes that Joyce offers a solution.[37]

Like Eliot, Döblin finds far more in *Ulysses* than allusions to the *Odyssey*. Disputing readings that emphasize only one aspect of the text, Döblin's review reinforces Eliot's assessment. Responding

---

[36] Breon Mitchell, *James Joyce and the German Novel, 1922–1933* (Athens, OH: Ohio University Press, 1976), 45.

[37] See also David Midgley, "The Dynamics of Consciousness: Alfred Döblin, *Berlin Alexanderplatz*," in *The German Novel in the Twentieth Century: Beyond Realism*, ed. David Midgley (Edinburgh: Edinburgh University Press, 1993), 97. Midgley emphasizes the review's praise for Joyce's realism: "When we find him describing Joyce's exactness of observation (in the Ithaca episode) as a 'scientific' style 'without an actual subject'; when he speaks of the expansion of the domain of literature to include the stuff of cinema and newspapers, and the restless discontinuities of city street impressions and modern traffic; when he insists that the heroic dimension of ancient epic has given way to the pervasive influence of economic and political systems, concluding that the contemporary sense of a 'crisis of the novel' merely reflects the fact that the mentalities of literary authors have not yet caught up with events—then we sense that this review is related to a debate about the modernisation of literature in which Döblin had been participating for many a year."

to a critic who called Joyce "the Homer of our day" (der Homer unserer Zeit), Döblin finds "no trace of Homer" (*keine Spur von einem Homer*).[38] At the same time, he finds "no trace of empty, dull naturalism" (*keine Spur von blankem, nüchternem Naturalismus*) (86). He disagrees with another critic who claimed the book was "a great tragedy" (*eine große Tragödie*) (85). Döblin's view is that *Ulysses* is comic and contemporary:

> It is, however, completely untragic, yet very powerful and crudely humourous, and is the most energetic attempt so far available in book form to squeeze the essence from modern, everyday life. For this pursuit, every fiction is completely discarded, and a minutely detailed and exact writing becomes necessary. It is worked impressionistically and pointilistically. It is not a question of combining grand, final ideas, whether internal or external. The connection between the individual, noticeable elements and moments establishes the association. This then is the method, and the book sends 1600 pages of signals concerning the 19-hour flow of life experiences of the three characters. (85–86)[39]

Döblin's observation that Joyce focuses on "individual, noticeable elements and moments" rather than "grand, final ideas" corresponds

---

[38] Alfred Döblin, "'Ulysses' von Joyce," *Das Deutsche Buch* 8 (1928): 84. My translation.

[39] Döblin writes: "Es ist aber ganz untragisch, sogar sehr kräftig und derb humoristisch und ist der energischste Versuch, dem heutigen Alltag auf den Leib zu rücken, der bisher in Buchform vorliegt. Zu diesem Versuch wird jede Fabel völlig abgeschüttelt, und es wird ein minutiöses Vorgehen im Detail nötig. Es wird impressionistisch und pointillistisch gearbeitet. Größere zusammenschließende Zielideen, äußere oder innere, kommen nicht in Frage. Die Verbindung zwischen den einzelnen aufnotierten Elementen und Momenten stellt die Assoziation her. Dies ist also die Methode, und das Buch gibt auf 1600 Seiten die Signale des 19stündigen Lebensablaufs der drei Personen."

to Roh's observation of postwar painters' preference for detail over summary and for miniature over monumental scale. Neither epic nor tragedy, neither naturalism nor abstraction, *Ulysses* is something entirely new:

> A second thing breaks through: now everything can be created anew. The lives of the three characters serve Joyce merely as a thread. Into these two days he incorporates an enormous sum of knowledge, allusions, moods, and fantasies. The book takes its name from that: "Ulysses" or an Odyssey through nearly all contemporary empirical experience, natural science and the arts. (86)[40]

This excess sustains multiple connections, and the incongruity of juxtaposed elements is ironic.

Eliot and Döblin regard duality as a fundamental quality in postwar art. Döblin claims: "The truly productive artist, however, must do two things: he must get up close to reality, to its objectivity, its blood, its smell, and then he has to break through the object, that is his specific task."[41] For Döblin, as for Roh, objectivity is the salient feature of the new art. Singling out the realistic plot as the unifying principle of *Ulysses*, Döblin reverses Eliot's assertion

---

[40] Döblin writes: "Es bricht etwas zweites durch: jetzt kann rechts und links neu 'gedichtet' werden. Das Leben der drei Personen dient Joyce nur als Faden. In diese zwei Tage baut er eine Unsumme von Wissen, Bibliotheksweisheit, Stimmungen und Phantasien ein. Von da hat das Buch seinen Namen: 'Ulysses' oder Odyssee fast der ganzen heutigen Empirie, Natur- und Geisteswissenschaft."

[41] Quoted by de Mendelssohn, *S. Fischer und sein Verlag*, 1174. Döblin writes: "Der wirklich Produktive aber muß zwei Schritte tun: er muß ganz nahe an die Realität heran, an ihre Sachlichkeit, ihr Blut, ihren Geruch, und dann hat er die Sache zu durchstoßen, das ist seine spezifische Arbeit."

that Joyce's use of the mythical was his great breakthrough. Just as Roh regards postwar painting as a departure from Expressionism, Döblin interprets the objectivity of *Ulysses* as a new direction in literature, but he fully agrees with Eliot's assessment of the impact that *Ulysses* will have on other writers. *Ulysses* may be inimitable, but it will change literature: "one does not have to do exactly what Joyce has done. There is no single way. This is an experimental work, neither a novel nor a poem, but a blow to their foundations."[42] By ignoring generic constraints, Joyce's method encompasses the full range of contemporary life: "It is a literary advance emerging from the conscience of modern-spirited people" (86).[43]

Ulysses showed Döblin that when history is a nightmare, realism is both inadequate and indispensable. This was also the lesson of postwar art. Döblin understood and imitated the fundamental irony produced by the diverse styles and tones of *Ulysses*. Undercutting the great ideas of the past, and treating serious matters comically and trivial matters seriously, *Ulysses* keeps meaning provisional. Döblin interprets *Ulysses* as a literary version of the combination of object and spirit in magic realist painting, and he implements Joyce's lessons in *Berlin Alexanderplatz*.

---

[42] Döblin, "'Ulysses' von Joyce," 85. Döblin writes: "… man muß es nicht so machen, wie es Joyce gemacht hat. Die Bahn ist nicht eingleisig. Dies ist ja auch ein Experimentierwerk, weder ein Roman noch eine Dichtung, sondern ein Beklopfen ihrer Grundelemente."

[43] Döblin writes: "Es ist ein literarischer Vorstoß aus dem Gewissen des heutigen geistigen Menschen heraus."

5

The German route from *Ulysses* to magic realism

The route from *Ulysses* to postcolonial magic realism is clearly marked, and it runs through Berlin. Echoing T. S. Eliot's claim that James Joyce made the modern world possible for art, in 1928 the German novelist Alfred Döblin praised *Ulysses* in similar terms: "It seeks, in its way, to answer the question: how can one write literature today? Above all, every serious writer has to deal with this book."[1] Döblin followed his own advice and revised the novel he was writing to incorporate Joyce's lessons.[2] When *Berlin Alexanderplatz: The Story of Franz Biberkopf* was published in 1929, it was immediately compared to *Ulysses*, yet

---

[1] Döblin, "'Ulysses' von Joyce," 86. Döblin writes: "Es sucht auf seine Weise die Frage zu beantworten: wie kann man heute dichten: Zunächst hat jeder ernste Schriftsteller sich mit diesem Buch zu befassen…." My translation.

[2] Mitchell, *James Joyce*, 133–34. Noting Döblin's "unhappiness with those critics who immediately pointed to Joyce in reviewing *Berlin Alexanderplatz*," Mitchell nevertheless points out that Döblin had written only a quarter of his novel when he reviewed *Ulysses*. Mitchell documents Joyce's influence on *Berlin Alexanderplatz* in detail and argues, "Joyce's work really is of great significance as a source for Döblin's volume. Just how much *Berlin Alexanderplatz* owes to *Ulysses* will become clear, I think, from the following close comparison of the original manuscript of the novel with the printed text."

it was also considered a prime example of the postwar movement variously known as New Objectivity and Magic Realism. In the words of one critic, "Döblin himself before long brought forth its most important realization."[3] The intersection of *Ulysses* and magic realism in *Berlin Alexanderplatz* leads to the familiar landmarks of the form that appeared after the Second World War.

Just as Döblin expressed his debt to Joyce, Günter Grass praised *Ulysses* for "the miracle of its language"[4] and said, "I come from Döblin."[5] Grass paid tribute to *Berlin Alexanderplatz* as "the masterpiece of an author whose every book I later used as a writing manual and in whose honor I created a prize."[6] Grass's response to the Second World War in *The Tin Drum* (1959, trans. 1961), in turn, stands behind Salman Rushdie's response to Indian Partition in *Midnight's Children* (1980). Rushdie honors Grass's protagonist by trying to "learn the lessons of the midget drummer" and compares his situation as a displaced Indian writer to "Joyce's abandoned Dublin" and "Grass's Danzig-become-Gdansk."[7] García Márquez joined this chorus in 2003, acknowledging that his account of the Colombian civil wars and US imperialism in *One Hundred Years of Solitude* (1967) was also made possible by *Ulysses*.[8]

---

[3] de Mendelssohn, *S. Fischer und sein Verlag*, 1092. My translation. Mendelssohn writes: "Döblin selbst brachte binnen kurzem ihre bedeutendste Verwirklichung hervor."
[4] Günter Grass, *Peeling the Onion*, trans. Michael Henry Heim (Orlando, FL: Harcourt, Inc. 2007), 387.
[5] Günter Grass, "Über meinen Lehrer Döblin und andere Vorträge," in *Alfred Döblin, 1878–1978*, ed. Jochen Meyer (Marbach am Neckar: Deutsche Schillergesellschaft, 1978), 520. My translation. He writes: "Ich komme von jenem Döblin her"
[6] Grass, *Peeling the Onion*, 387.
[7] Salman Rushdie, *Imaginary Homelands* (London: Granta Books, 1991), 277 and 15.
[8] Gabriel García Márquez, *Living to Tell the Tale*, trans. Edith Grossman (New York: Alfred A. Knopf, 2003), 247.

The purpose of retracing the path from Joyce to the end of the century is not to add Joyce and Döblin to the ever-increasing ranks of magic realist authors but to argue that all these writers used similar strategies because they faced the same problem: how to represent the unimaginable violence of their times in a secular age.[9] Joyce's solution was to construct arbitrary relationships between realistic events and multiple symbolic patterns, thus maintaining the structure of meaning without endorsing any particular meaning. In addition, he introduced a type of irony that is based on formal incongruities rather than on a disparity between what speakers say and what they mean. But irony can be hard to hear when it touches the reader's beliefs. By pointing out the ironic combination of realism and symbolism in *Ulysses* and the texts it influenced, I hope to amplify the irony in all of them. Although there are significant differences between early and late examples of magic realism, Joyce's successors adopted his strategies for bearing witness to the nightmares of history.

---

[9] On Joyce as a formative precursor of postcolonial magic realism, see Morton B. Levitt, *Modernist Survivors* (Columbus: Ohio State University Press, 1987); Declan Kiberd, "James Joyce and Mythic Realism," in *The Regional Novel in Britain and Ireland, 1800–1990*, ed. K.D.M. Snell (Cambridge: Cambridge University Press, 1998), 152–53. Kiberd writes that Joyce "was, by virtue of his location, a leader of European modernism: but, by virtue of his example, he became a pioneer of mythical realism." Kiberd locates *Ulysses* on a continuum: "The modernism of Joyce was not only that of Mann, Proust or Eliot: it also anticipated that of Rushdie, Márquez and the post-colonial artists." Reserving the term "magic realism" for later postcolonial writers, Kiberd regards Joyce's "canny blend of myth and realism" as a prototype of subversive magic realism: "He was one of the earliest writers to realise that as long as he posed his questions to the west solely in the old, familiar terms of the west, he would be surrendering to the ends of its discourse, just as to resort to pure fabulism, untouched by any element of realism, would be to submit to the intentions of the native tribe. Mythic realism, by its subversive act of combination, disrupted the hegemony of both discourses so that neither could achieve its goals."

Criticism of these texts illustrates how easy it is for readers to become tone deaf when the text speaks to their personal convictions. For example, Bloom's speech about love in the "Cyclops" episode of *Ulysses* is generally taken as a sincere statement of authorial meaning. While this view has textual support, readers' values filter the evidence. John Nash observes that although "Cyclops" parodies the nationalist discourse of the first-person narrator as well as Irish legends, myths, and newspaper prose, Bloom's idea of love is rarely read as parody.[10] Analyzing readings that take Bloom as the fixed point of meaning, Nash observes that critics fall into "false dichotomies" (179) between what is ironic and what is genuine. In contrast, Nash argues that "no single character or language-use holds a voice of authority that fully escapes the parody" (179). Parody does not cancel all meaning, but "reading 'Cyclops' demands reading with both eyes the ebb and flow of the text" (179).

For most critics, however, the irony of "Cyclops" stops when Bloom tries to convince the chauvinist citizen that "insult and hatred" are not "really life"; what matters, he says, is love, "the opposite of hatred."[11] But this noble affirmation is immediately undercut. First, the citizen mocks Bloom, "—A new apostle to the gentiles, says the citizen. Universal love" (273). He reduces Bloom's definition of love as an ethical imperative to selfish passion: "Beggar my neighbour is his motto. Love, moya! He's a nice pattern of a Romeo and Juliet" (273). This rejoinder can be discounted as the citizen's contempt, but it is

---

[10] John Nash, "'Hanging over the bloody paper': Newspapers and Imperialism in *Ulysses*," in *Modernism and Empire*, ed. Howard J. Booth and Nigel Rigby (Manchester and New York: Manchester University Press, 2000), 176.
[11] James Joyce, *Ulysses*, 273.

followed by a free-floating riff on love. An unidentified speaker who knows more than the narrator of the episode or any of the characters minimizes the emotions that Bloom and the citizen express in direct speech. "Love" occupies every syntactic position:

> Love loves to love love. Nurse loves the new chemist. Constable 14 A loves Mary Kelly. Gerty MacDowell loves the boy that has the bicycle. M. B. loves a fair gentleman. Li Chi Han lovey up kissy Cha Pu Chow. Jumbo, the elephant, loves Alice, the elephant. Old Mr Verschoyle with the ear trumpet loves old Mrs Verschoyle with the turnedin eye. The man in the brown macintosh loves a lady who is dead. His Majesty the King loves Her Majesty the Queen. Mrs Norman W. Tupper loves officer Taylor. You love a certain person. And this person loves that other person because everybody loves somebody but God loves everybody. (273)[12]

Repetition almost reduces the first sentence to doggerel, though it can be construed as an expression of the narcissism of love. The list of lovers exceeds the consciousness of any single character. Only readers and Gerty MacDowell know that she loves the boy with a bicycle. Bloom has been thinking about Molly and her lover all day but never as "M. B." The Chinese couple and the elephants appear

---

[12] See Karen Lawrence, *The Odyssey of Style in "Ulysses"* (Princeton, NJ: Princeton University Press, 1981), 115. Lawrence argues that Joyce's parody in this passage represents the "inadequacy of language to convey *emotion*; the language of feeling has degenerated into sentimental cant." See also Paul B. Armstrong, *Play and the Politics of Reading: The Social Uses of Modernist Form* (Ithaca and London: Cornell University Press, 2005), 148–59. Armstrong argues that the "irony in *Ulysses* is often difficult to read, sometimes because of the inability of any position in a contingent world to justify itself absolutely, but sometimes because Joyce seems to seek through irony to evade responsibility for and involvement in the dilemmas he points out ironically" (151).

nowhere else. The range of examples trivializes love for all of them. Even the reassuring counterexample, "God loves everybody," becomes a platitude at the end of a chain of unreciprocated loves. The series belongs to a collective consciousness that the text constructs. Using Bloom's sacred word in a comic list of lovers, this paragraph erodes his moral authority. However sincerely Bloom may believe that love can overcome hatred, the disparity between his belief and the tone of this paragraph should warn readers not to attribute equal sincerity to the author.

The episode culminates in an act of trivial violence. When Bloom proclaims, "Christ was a jew like me" (280), the Citizen throws a biscuit box at him. The ordinary object generates inflated responses on all fronts. Bloom's departure is narrated in biblical pastiche that describes his escape as an apotheosis:

> When, lo, there came about them all a great brightness and they beheld the chariot wherein He stood ascend to heaven ... And they beheld Him even Him, ben Bloom Elijah, amid clouds of angels ascend to the glory of the brightness at an angle of fortyfive degrees over Donohoe's in Little Green street like a shot off a shovel. (282–83)

Religious hyperbole fizzles into the homely simile that ends the episode. The passage combines biblical phrases and clichés, the supernatural feats of miracle and the empirical details of measurement and place. Invoking supernatural events ironically, the text denies their credibility but preserves their symbolic effect.

Irony allows Joyce to address the issue of political violence without supporting partisans or pacifists. The scene portrays nationalism, ethnic chauvinism, and anti-Semitism but does not attempt to explain their causes or show their more serious consequences. Bloom's miraculous transformation anticipates the fantastic events that generate symbolic meanings in later magic realist texts, which also use religious discourse to convey secular ideas. No one interprets Bloom's ascension as a supernatural event, yet the comparable ascension of Remedios the Beauty in *One Hundred Years of Solitude* is often understood as a sign of postcolonial spirituality.[13]

Like Bloom's speech about love, Franz Biberkopf's rebirth at the end of *Berlin Alexanderplatz* is usually understood as a validation of authorial belief, but Döblin undercuts every statement of meaning. In 1920, he had published *Wallenstein*, which transmuted his combat experience in the First World War into a historical novel about the Thirty Years' War. In addition to implying parallels between the two wars, *Wallenstein* is modeled on *Der abenteuerliche Simplicissimus* by Hans Jakob Christoffel von Grimmelshausen.[14] While writing *Berlin Alexanderplatz* about the aftermath of the war, however, Döblin read *Ulysses* and adopted many of its strategies. Neither novel portrays warfare, but both scrutinize violence. Although both novels are often interpreted as vividly realistic or deeply symbolic,[15] they unite

---

[13] For a recent example, see Persephone Braham, *From Amazons to Zombies: Monsters in Latin America* (Lewisburg: Bucknell University Press, 2015), 172.

[14] Jameson, "War and Representation," 1537–42.

[15] See, for example, Virginia Woolf, "Modern Fiction," in *The Common Reader* (New York: Harcourt, Brace & World, 1953), 155. Woolf praises *Ulysses* as a corrective to the realism of Bennett, Wells, and Galsworthy: "In contrast with those whom we have called materialists Mr. Joyce is spiritual." See also Ezra Pound, "Ulysses," in *Literary Essays of Ezra Pound*, ed. T. S. Eliot (New York: New Directions, 1968), 407. Pound considers the novel realistic: "He has presented Ireland under British domination, a picture so veridic that a ninth rate coward like Shaw (Geo. B.) dare not even look it in the face." For Döblin, see Midgley,

sensory experience with ideas and emotions that have no empirical foundation.

Berlin Alexanderplatz exaggerates the pastiche of discourses of *Ulysses*, producing a similar kind of formal irony. Döblin imitates the Bible, government reports, popular songs, street slang, Greek epic, newspapers, sentimental fiction, and scientific treatises. The exuberant cacophony of voices creates an ironic distance from Franz Biberkopf's inarticulate struggle to survive in postwar Berlin. All the speakers, including first-person narrators, are disengaged from the events and characters they describe. For example, Franz's fatal beating of his girlfriend is reported in the language of physics:

> What happened to the woman's diaphragm a second before, involves the laws of statics, elasticity, shock, and resistance. The thing is wholly incomprehensible without a knowledge of those laws. We shall therefore have recourse to the following formulae:
>
> Newton's first law which says: Every body perseveres in its state of rest or of moving uniformly in a straight line, except so far as it is made to change that state by external force (this applies to Ida's ribs).[16]

"The Dynamics of Consciousness," 107. Midgley summarizes a similar division among critics of *Berlin Alexanderplatz*: "If the published commentaries on *Berlin Alexanderplatz* contradict each other in many respects, then that is because the commentators have tended to emphasise particular aspects of Döblin's work over others, according to their own predisposition. [Some] emphasise the spiritual dimension over the material…. [Others emphasise] the material dimension by focusing on Biberkopf's contest with society in the form of the big city, … the strand of political anarchism in Döblin's outlook—opposed to the centralised state, opposed to the political machinery of big parties." He concludes, "Whatever might be said for each individual line of interpretation, the text does not permit any one of them finally to dominate over the others."

[16] Alfred Döblin, *Berlin Alexanderplatz: The Story of Franz Biberkopf*, trans. Eugene Jolas (New York: Frederick Ungar Publishing Co., 1931), 123–24.

The parody of scientific discourse mocks its pretensions to objectivity and accuracy. Knowledge of physics does nothing to make Franz's violence less "incomprehensible." The novel's discordant discourses and disparities between tone and events prevent readers from construing any consistent authorial position. As in *Ulysses*, there are innumerable possible meanings, but there is no stable point of view to guide interpretive choices.

Yet many critics take Franz's rebirth as a socialist worker seriously, assuming that irony ends when he reforms. For example, David B. Dollenmayer argues that Franz "is not destroyed by an inevitable fate, but is redeemed through his final realization of guilt, responsibility for his own life, and dependence on others."[17] Dollenmayer believes that the conversion "with its echoes of biblical diction, suggests that Biberkopf's end is modelled on a Christian rather than a Greek worldview" (84). Or perhaps a Christian Socialist worldview, since Biberkopf discovers the benefits of solidarity: "As we have seen, the social is linked to the personal at the point where Biberkopf realizes he cannot stand alone, but must live among and depend upon his fellow men in the city and in life in general" (87). There is textual evidence for this view. After denying any responsibility for his violent crimes, Franz finally says: "I'm guilty, I'm not a human being, I'm just a beast, a monster" (617), and a first-person narrator affirms that Franz is reborn: "Thus died, in that evening hour, Franz Biberkopf, erstwhile transport-worker, burglar, pimp, murderer" (617). The narrator continues, "Now I will append a report about the first hours and days of a new man, having the same identity papers as he" (617).

---

[17] David B. Dollenmayer, *The Berlin Novels of Alfred Döblin* (Berkeley: University of California Press, 1988), 84.

The report, however, does not show much change: "Now Biberkopf is back again: your Biberkopf is back again" (624). The new Franz does exactly what the old Franz did: "And then what does he do? He starts little by little to go about the streets, he walks around Berlin" (625). He gets a job as "assistant door-man in a medium sized factory" (632), and a narrator moralizes: "Much unhappiness comes from walking alone. When there are several, it's somewhat different. I must get the habit of listening to others, for what the others say concerns me, too. Then I learn who I am, and what I can undertake" (633). But Döblin does not allow socialist solidarity to expiate Franz's crimes. One moment he renounces "walking alone," and the next he separates himself from marching masses: "Biberkopf watches coolly from his door, he'll not join the parade any more.... But if I march along, I shall have to pay for it later on with my head, pay for the schemes of others. That's why I first figure out everything, and only if everything's quite O. K., and suits me, I'll take action" (633–34). Franz's inability to sustain his social consciousness mocks the text's claims that he is a new man.

The voice of socialism is no more reliable than any other voice. First-person speakers offer spurious summations throughout the novel. Socialism is merely the last in a series of discarded sources of meaning, including religion, military ideals, nationalism, literature, and Freudian psychology. The text's use of socialist rhetoric does not indicate political conviction any more than its biblical discourse implies religious belief. The extraordinary change in Franz can symbolize a conversion to Christianity or socialism or any other system of belief. The only constant among many possibilities is that the apparent conversion is a temporary change. Like Bloom's apotheosis,

Franz's rebirth illustrates how an ironic account of an extreme event can offer multiple explanations without endorsing any of them.

The mixture of extremity, excess, and irony in *Ulysses* and *Berlin Alexanderplatz* proved useful to writers facing a similar aesthetic crisis after the Second World War. Just as Theodor Adorno reiterated the despair of the 1920s when he remarked that to write poetry after Auschwitz was barbaric, writers in the second half of the century found a way out of this impasse in the art produced after the First World War. They continued to combine historical realism and transhistorical symbolism ironically, but after the Second World War, writers raised the voltage to signal symbolic meaning. Grass, García Márquez, and Rushdie produce formal irony by reversing the narrative conventions of symbolism and realism: historical events are incredible, and supernatural occurrences are ordinary. Fantastic events are described in abundant empirical detail, while supernatural claims and allusions are attached to historical events. Atrocities are minimized, and trivial events are exaggerated.

Instead of imitating cultural discourses as Joyce and Döblin do, Grass focalizes the narrative of *The Tin Drum* through Oskar and then destabilizes this point of view. The magic realist conceit that Oskar, the primary narrator, is a child with "clairaudient" powers allows him to observe events before, during, and after the war from a naïve perspective.[18] Oskar speaks of himself as "I" and "he." At times, he turns the narrative over to Bruno, his attendant in the mental hospital where the narrative begins. Oskar's style and tone

---

[18] Günter Grass, *The Tin Drum*, trans. Breon Mitchell (Boston and New York: Houghton Mifflin Harcourt, 2010), 35.

are inconsistent and often unsuited to his situation. In homage to *Ulysses*, Grass alludes to the musical structure of "Sirens" in "Faith Hope Love," and he echoes the catechism style of "Ithaca" in "Bebra's Theater at the Front": "Why did Oskar put his sailor's cap with the flowing ribbon back on again and stride away capped? Because he had an appointment at the Langfuhr freight-train station. Did he arrive on time at the appointed spot? He did" (305). The dramatic form of "Circe" stands behind Grass's scriptlike account of Oskar's visit to the German fortifications on the Normandy coast in "Inspecting Concrete—or Mystical Barbaric Bored." Grass even has Oskar disingenuously protest that he is not "a modern-day Ulysses"; he will not start "bandying about names like Circe, Penelope, and Telemachus the minute he gets home" (327).

But Grass is more explicit about the function of irony and symbolism than Joyce is. Oskar recounts his personal autobiography as an allegory of public events. He invents explanations of historical crises, positing ironic parallels among military battles, domestic disputes, magical feats, and literary antecedents. For example, he says: "I hope you will indulge me if I draw a parallel between the mud-logged victories of Army Group Center and my victories in the trackless and equally muddy terrain of Frau Lina Greff" (287). The complicity that sustains the erotic ménage of his mother, father, and uncle corresponds to the "Triple Alliance" of Germany, Austria–Hungary, and Italy (44). His glass-shattering voice could have "replaced several high-caliber machine guns" and "instilled a belief in miracle weapons right from the start of the war, but it would not have saved the Polish Post Office" (207). All the characters are thoroughly idiosyncratic, yet they represent political opponents.

Oskar has German and Polish relatives, and he is befriended by Nazis and Jews.

The fantastic events in the novel are clearly symbolic, though Grass assimilates magic to realistic situations. Oskar acquires multiple mothers, fathers, and cultural avatars as he recounts a series of ordinary and fantastic experiences. Endowed with preternatural knowledge at birth, Oskar decides to stop growing when he reaches the age of three; his mother, however, attributes his smallness to a fall down the cellar stairs. Oskar uses his magical powers to drum and scream for his personal benefit, yet these powers also evoke the historical significance of military drums and victims' screams:

> The ability to drum up the necessary distance between grownups and myself on a toy drum developed soon after my fall down the cellar stairs, almost simultaneously with the emergence of a voice that allowed me to sing, scream, or sing-scream at such a high pitch and with such sustained vibrato that no one dared take away the drum that pained their ears; for when my drum was taken from me I screamed, and when I screamed something quite valuable would burst into pieces: I was able to singshatter glass. (52)

Oskar's scream has the supernatural power to break glass windows as well as the earthly benefit of manipulating adults. Oskar's drum is both a toy and a symbol. His riff on drums demonstrates the multiplicity of symbolic meanings:

> We have eardrums and brake drums, we drum up excuses, drum into our heads, drum out of the corps .... I might mention Tattoos, both minor and major, and Oskar's attempts up to now: all that is nothing compared with the orgy of drumming staged

by that moth with two simple sixty-watt bulbs on the day of my birth. (36)

The signifier "drum" generates all these associations to empirical and nonempirical referents. Regardless of the use of the object itself, the play of the signifier in this chain permits the substitutions that constitute symbolic meaning.

Connecting symbolic meanings to empirical reality, Oskar embodies the magic realist aesthetic that Roh articulates. Like magic realist paintings, Oskar is miniature—he decides to stop growing at age three, retaining the child's status as bystander rather than responsible witness. As a child, he is exempt from the duty to make judgments, though he generalizes that to be human is to be "childlike, curious, complex, immoral" (68). Oskar's size allows Grass to associate him with real and imaginary "little people" such as "Little Hans," "Hop-o'-My-Thumb," "the gnome," and "Tom Thumb" (48). His adventures crisscross the boundary between the animate and the inanimate. He feels that he is "being watched by the furniture and the light bulb" (472). His mother's eyes "seem accustomed to regarding the souls of her fellow beings, as well as her own, as solid objects—a coffee cup, say, or a cigarette holder" (43).

Going further than Roh, Grass initiates a transition from the connection between object and spirit in magic realism to the meaning of things in themselves in thing theory. Oskar not only invests his drum with meanings, but he regards it as an animate being. The toy is a thing with a life of its own. It speaks, it remembers, and it acts in the world. It "recalls all the little details" of the past (13), and it is the "lacquered, red-flamed conscience round my neck" that tells him what to do (242). When his mother dies, he overhears his grandmother blame him: "My Agnes died because she couldn't stand the drumming no more" (159). If his drum causes her death, it also consoles him:

> Even if I did cause my poor mama's death, I clung all the more tightly to my despised drum, for it didn't die as a mother does, you could buy a new one, have it repaired by old man Heilandt or Laubschad the clockmaker, it understood me, always gave the right answer, it stuck with me, and I stuck with it. (159)

Oskar's drum imparts meaning. It is a companion that does not die. After Oskar wears out a drum, he numbers it, stores it the cellar, and demands a new drum, which functions exactly like the old one. But when he temporarily lacks a drum, he beats on a tin can: "This misguided attempt cured me forever. Never again did I make a serious effort to use a tin can, an overturned bucket, or a washtub bottom as a drum" (196). He refuses to accept a substitute: "A tin can is no tin drum, a bucket is a bucket, and a washtub is for washing yourself or your socks. Just as there's no substitute today, there was none back then; a tin drum with red and white flames speaks for itself and needs no spokesman" (196). Each object has its own purpose, its own meaning. This singularity acquires ethical significance. Oskar comes to see that symbols allow him to evade reality and responsibility. He distinguishes object from symbol to separate fact from lie. All too aware of the extravagant meanings of symbols, he resolves to put an end to indeterminacy. When he is ready to accept responsibility for his actions, he renounces the meaning of his drum as a symbol: "I can never silence that inner voice, be it ever so plaintive: It was my drum, no, it was I myself, Oskar the drummer, who sent first my poor mama, then Jan Bronski, my uncle and father, to the grave" (230). Although he is tempted to blame their deaths on his drum, he assumes the burden of guilt.

The meaning of the novel is indeterminate, but Oskar points out the ethical weakness of indeterminacy. He turns to things for the order that beliefs no longer provide. Things are more reliable than people:

> Today I know that all things are watching, that nothing goes unseen, that even wallpaper has a better memory than human beings. It's not God in his heaven who sees everything. A kitchen chair, a clothes hanger, a half-filled ashtray, or the wooden replica of a woman named Niobe can serve perfectly well as an unforgetting witness to our every deed. (177)

Objects do not last, but they are better witnesses than anything divine or human. Neither God nor people can be expected to bear witness to events. Neither divine nor communal meaning is available. For Oskar, the material world is not merely a source of symbolic objects; it has agency.

Grass dramatizes the problem of representing violence in art by creating a number of characters who are artists—painters, sculptors, musicians, circus performers, and magicians. Lankes, for example, uses the German army's pillboxes on the Normandy coast as a medium for art. Anticipating postwar acclaim, he imagines that a viewer will "see my structurally oblique formations, and say to himself: Let's have a look at this. Interesting. One might almost say magical; menacing, yet imbued with striking spirituality" (318). His aesthetic echoes half of Roh's definition of magic realism. Bebra, Oskar's mentor, underlines the symbolic meaning of the title Lankes gives his work:

LANKES: All right, here's what it says: Herbert Lankes, anno nineteen hundred and forty-four. Title: MYSTICAL, BARBARIC, BORED.

BEBRA: You have given our century its name. (318)

Lankes's art seems "mystical" because it is abstract, but it lacks the irony and specificity of magic realism. He uses abstraction to evade responsibility. He and Oskar return to the pillboxes after the war. The site of military violence becomes a scene of personal violence when Lankes rapes a young nun who happens to be on the beach gathering seashells. His crime inspires him to paint a "whole series of nuns" (526). He reprises the title of his war art for one of his canvases: "Black, lots of black, dead white, and cold-storage blue: The Invasion, or Mystical, Barbaric, Bored" (526). Presenting the abstract images as symbols of the war, Lankes expresses yet conceals his own violence. His paintings register the devolution of abstraction from Expressionist representations of spiritual fullness to late-century desolation.

Oskar is a different kind of artist. As he considers possible methods of representing the Nazis' invasion of Poland, he weighs poetic symbolism against documentary realism:

I hope you'll forgive Oskar for adding this final couplet and for the poetic nature of the battle scene. I might have done better to indicate the number of men lost by the Polish cavalry, and commemorate the so-called Polish Campaign with dry but impressive statistics. But if asked, I could introduce an asterisk here, add a footnote, and let the poem stand. (234)

Instead of choosing, he follows the path of Joyce and Döblin and offers both statistics and a poem.

When Grass's 2007 memoir *Peeling the Onion* revealed that he had been a member of the SS, public outrage targeted the indeterminacy of meaning in his fiction. Suddenly Grass seemed more like Lankes than like Oskar. Grass's memoir, however, describes the same aesthetic problem that other twentieth-century writers faced. Attempting to convey his first experience of combat, Grass rejected the obvious models:

> But I had already read everything I write here. I had read it in Remarque or Céline, who—like Grimmelshausen before them in his description of the Battle of Wittstock, when the Swedes hacked the Kaiser's troops to pieces—were merely quoting the scenes of horror handed down to them.[19]

The nightmares of the Second World War seemed impossible to represent: "Nor could I bear to come out with things long lurking within me: the questions I had failed to ask... the disbelief at the pictures of Bergen-Belsen, at the piles of corpses—look at them, go ahead look at them, don't turn away, just because—to put it mildly—

---

[19] Grass, *Peeling the Onion*, 125. Grass does not mention his "teacher" Alfred Döblin's use of Grimmelshausen in *Wallenstein*, written during the First World War. See also Jameson, "War and Representation," 1537. Jameson cites Grimmelshausen's account of the "nightmares" of the Thirty Years' War, but in contrast to Grass's view that it is a conventional inventory of atrocities, Jameson cites it as an example of later representations of war that eliminate human agents to focus on the impact of violence on the "scene" or landscape.

it is beyond description" (285–86). His solution was to turn to the oblique method of *Ulysses* and the specificity of magic realism: "What does memory cling to? A still life with a practical goal and no pretensions to art" (120). He endorses Roh's tribute to the truth of things: "Found objects, which, when invoked with sufficient intensity, will begin to reveal their mysteries" (54). Things contain meanings.

Although *The Tin Drum* is widely recognized as a precursor of *Midnight's Children*, the prevailing critical view is that magic realism is a postcolonial genre. This consensus stems from Alejo Carpentier's claim in 1949 that Latin American writers had a natural connection to an extraordinary world that he called *lo real maravilloso*. Carpentier argued that whereas Europeans had to create the marvelous, Latin Americans found it readymade throughout their history and geography: "After all, what is the entire history of America if not a chronicle of the marvelous real?"[20] García Márquez's *One Hundred Years of Solitude* is probably the salient example of magic realism today, and it seems to epitomize Carpentier's claim. García Márquez himself emphasized the indigenous roots of the novel, telling an interviewer in 1973 that it was based on his childhood: "My grandmother used to tell me stories and my grandfather took

---

[20] Alejo Carpentier, "On the Marvelous Real in America," in *Magical Realism: Theory, History, Community*, ed. Lois Parkinson Zamora and Wendy B. Faris (Durham and London: Duke University Press, 1995), 88. Although Carpentier speaks as a native, he lived in Paris from 1928 to 1939. As he says, only when he returned home did Latin America seem marvelous: "The Latin American returns to his own world and begins to understand many things" (83). See also Alejo Carpentier, "The Baroque and the Marvelous Real," in *Magical Realism: Theory, History, Community*, ed. Lois Parkinson Zamora and Wendy B. Faris (Durham and London: Duke University Press, 1995), 102. Carpentier erroneously dismisses Franz Roh's concept of magic realism by calling it "simply Expressionist painting" (102), though Roh's book had been available in Spanish since 1927.

me to see things. Those were the circumstances in which my world was constructed."[21] In a 1979 essay on Latin American writing, he virtually echoed Carpentier: "In Latin America and the Caribbean artists have had to invent very little, and perhaps they have had the opposite problem: to make their reality believable ... the reality they encountered surpassed imagination."[22]

But reality that surpasses imagination turns out to resemble history that is a nightmare. García Márquez calls attention to this resemblance in his 2003 memoir *Living to Tell the Tale*. Here he distances himself from Carpentier and takes a more cosmopolitan stance. He names *Ulysses* the "other Bible" of his generation of Latin American writers. The book "not only was the discovery of a genuine world that I never suspected inside me, but it also provided invaluable technical help to me in freeing language and in handling time and structures in my books."[23] He learned that a story did not have to be realistic to be credible:

It was not necessary to demonstrate facts: it was enough for the author to have written something for it to be true, with no proof other than the power of his talent and the authority of his voice. It was Scheherazade all over again, not in her millenary world where everything was possible but in another irreparable world where everything had already been lost. (247–48)

[21] Rita Guibert, "Gabriel García Márquez," in *Seven Voices: Seven Latin American Writers Talk to Rita Guibert*, trans. Frances Partridge (New York: Alfred A. Knopf, 1973), 323.
[22] Gabriel García Márquez, "Fantasía y creación artística en América Latina y el Caribe," *Texto crítico* 14 (Jul–Sept 1979): 4. My translation. He writes: "En América Latina y el Caribe los artistas han tenido que inventar muy poco, y tal vez su problema ha sido el contrario: hacer creíble su realidad .... se encontraron con que la realidad iba más lejos que la imaginación."
[23] García Márquez, *Living to Tell the Tale*, 247.

This is the world all twentieth-century writers faced, and it was defined by political violence. As García Márquez states, "I believe I had become aware that on April 9, 1948, the twentieth century began in Colombia" (303). On that date, the leader of the opposition to the Conservative government was assassinated, precipitating riots and military rule. García Márquez had to find a way to write about massacres, and he credited Joyce with demonstrating how a new kind of narrative could represent a world of violence and loss.

Almost every critical discussion of magic realism begins with a defense of one of these points of origin: Europe after the First World War or Latin America after the Second World War. Seymour Menton labels the two positions the Internationalist and the Americanist. While Internationalists emphasize the continuity of the form, Americanists distinguish European magic realism from *lo real maravilloso*, a form rooted in the "mythological elements in its Indian and African substrata."[24] The stakes in this debate are political as well as literary. If Internationalists minimize the distinctive cultural sources of postcolonial fiction, Americanists build their case on regionalist assumptions. Conflating political and epistemological arguments, Americanists contend that magic realism resists the hegemony of European imperialism as expressed in realism, science, and reason and that it advances postcolonial identity as expressed

---

[24] Seymour Menton, "Magic Realism: An Annotated International Chronology of the Term" in *Essays in Honor of Frank Dauster*, ed. Kirsten F. Nigro and Sandra M. Cypess (Newark, DE: Juan de la Cuesta, 1995), 126. See also Seymour Menton, *Magic Realism Rediscovered, 1918–1981* (Philadelphia: Art Alliance Press and Associated University Presses, 1983), 13. Menton argues that magic realism is a valid term for both visual and literary art from the end of the First World War to the present: "The oxymoronic combination of *realism* and *magic* captures the artists' and the authors' efforts to portray the strange, the uncanny, the eerie, and the dreamlike—but not the fantastic—aspects of everyday reality."

in myth, indigenous traditions, and religious beliefs. This critical disjunction perpetuates a series of dichotomies between the material and the spiritual, the individual and the collective, and the personal and the political, as if stories and facts, mythos and logos, did not exist in every culture.

The Americanist view has come to dominate criticism of magic realism. For example, in *Mimesis, Genres and Post-Colonial Discourse: Deconstructing Magic Realism*, Jean-Pierre Durix repeats Carpentier's regionalist claims about *lo real maravilloso*: "Where, in European literature, the fantastic serves to protest against the tyranny of 'fact', in post-colonial literature it frequently serves to incorporate the old values and beliefs into the modern man's perception. It has a social function, whereas in European literature, it more often expresses individualistic rebellion."[25] Wendy B. Faris, coeditor of the influential anthology of criticism *Magical Realism: Theory, History, Community*, makes the same point in her subsequent book, *Ordinary Enchantments: Magical Realism and the Remystification of Narrative*. Although she cites *One Hundred Years of Solitude*, *The Tin Drum*, and *Midnight's Children* as "definitive" examples,[26] she regards magic realism as a "shamanistic" form (75), arguing that it provides a "possible remystification of narrative in the West" that could

---

[25] Jean-Pierre Durix, *Mimesis, Genres and Post-Colonial Discourse: Deconstructing Magic Realism* (New York: St. Martin's Press, Inc., 1998), 81.

[26] Wendy B. Faris, *Ordinary Enchantments: Magical Realism and the Remystification of Narrative* (Nashville: Vanderbilt University Press, 2004), 29. See also Brian Conniff, "The Dark Side of Magical Realism: Science, Oppression, and Apocalypse in *One Hundred Years of Solitude*," *Modern Fiction Studies* 36 (1990): 168. Coniff believes that magic realism owes its popularity to readers' desire to believe in something: "'Magical realism' has typically been seen as the redemption of fiction in the face of a reality that is still becoming progressively more disorderly."

"reverse the progressive secularization" of contemporary culture (65). She claims that "a common and often noted factor in much magical realist fiction is the tapping of belief systems that predate the Enlightenment" (70), and she believes that the form reveals "the inadequacy of scientifically based perspectives and forms of discourse" (83). Magic realism can even redeem historical violence: "Magical realism not only reflects history ..., it may also seek to change it, by addressing historical issues critically and thereby attempting to heal historical wounds" (138). She understands magic realism as an expression of the "ineffable":

> From a philosophical perspective, the irreducible element forms a counterweight to empiricism; from a narratological perspective, it represents a new kind of focalization; and from a religious perspective, it constitutes an incipient re-emergence of spirit or the sacred. (68)

Faris invests magic realism with spiritual power, making it a postmodern substitute for religion, a source of positive belief, rather than a symbolic literary form open to many interpretations.

The fantastic events in postcolonial examples of magic realism are more likely to be read as evidence of belief than those in European texts. Christopher Warnes notes that the supernatural in postcolonial fiction is often understood as a way "to reconcile the modern, rational, 'disenchanted' subject of the West with forgotten but recoverable spiritual realities."[27] Some novels that are considered magic realist

---

[27] Christopher Warnes, "Naturalizing the Supernatural: Faith, Irreverence and Magical Realism," *Literature Compass* 2 (2005): 1.

do fit this regionalist paradigm. Carpentier's *Kingdom of This World*, Juan Rulfo's *Pedro Páramo*, and Ben Okri's *The Famished Road*, for example, are not ironic. They realistically depict characters who believe in supernatural powers. The harmony between a sincere narrative tone and characters' beliefs invites readers to attribute credulity not just to characters but to members of the culture that the characters represent. The beliefs in other postcolonial texts, however, are not as authentic as Western readers often assume. Warnes distinguishes between "an attitude of *faith* and one of *irreverence* in magical realist writing" (2), tracing the former attitude to Alejo Carpentier and the latter to Jorge Luis Borges (5). Borges's "irreverence" underlies the irony that Warnes perceives in García Márquez and Rushdie (11).

In addition to writers' attitudes, readers' preconceptions determine whether a text is interpreted as an expression of faith or irreverence. *One Hundred Years of Solitude* illustrates how a single text can seem sincere to some readers and ironic to others. Although most critics emphasize its spirituality, readers who are more familiar with the historical context of the novel read it as an ironic political critique.[28] Lucila Inés Mena, for example, considers it the culmination of the novel of violence, a form that emerged in Colombia in response to the political wars of the 1940s and 1950s. Mena values the indirect

---

[28] See Gene H. Bell-Villada, "García Márquez and the Novel," *Latin American Literary Review* 13 (January–June 1985): 20. Bell-Villada points out the political meaning of magical events in the work of García Márquez: "For paradoxically the unreality in García Márquez, while intended for the delectation of readers who do in fact enjoy the wild invention for its own sake, actually has the hidden job of underscoring and enhancing the realities under depiction. Hence the priest levitates because he seeks contributions for a brand-new church and knows that a miracle will impress the villagers." In brief, "The hyperbole of the book, while unforgettable, again exaggerates from real-life facts" (23).

approach of *One Hundred Years of Solitude* because it uncovers the "roots of violence." The effort "to give a literary reality to political violence," she writes, required more than an "inventory of corpses" [29] Similarly, Regina Janes calls attention to a little-known newspaper article García Márquez wrote in 1959 titled "Dos o tres cosas sobre 'la novela de la violencia'" (Two or Three Things about the "Novel of Violence") in which he argues that it is more important to express the "atmosphere" that leads to violence than to describe atrocities realistically. Janes comments, "The final, fitting irony of the episode [the massacre of banana workers] is that North American readers unfamiliar with the history of Colombia assume that the episode is one more fantastic invention."[30] Hearing the irony in the narrative, these critics do not regard *One Hundred Years of Solitude* as a re-enchantment of narrative but as a recuperation of the writer's ability to represent unimaginable violence.

García Márquez's article analyzes the difficulty of representing violence. Despite his leftist political views, García Márquez rejects the

---

[29] Lucila Inés Mena, "Bibliografía anotada sobre el ciclo de la violencia en la literatura colombiana," *Latin American Research Review* 13 (1978): 98–99. My translation.

[30] Regina Janes, "Liberals, Conservatives, and Bananas: Colombian Politics in the Fictions of Gabriel García Márquez," in *Gabriel García Márquez*, ed. Harold Bloom (New York: Chelsea House, 1989), 140. Janes summarizes the argument of "Dos o tres cosas sobre la novela de la violencia": "García Márquez discussed the problem of treating contemporary political issues in fiction and defined the way he was to handle them in his earlier works. The fault he found with most novels dealing with 'la violencia' was that they were bad novels, and they were bad in large part because the novelists had forgotten that novels must deal with the living and not with the dead. They had put 'la violencia' first and gone astray in descriptions 'de los decapitados, de los castrados, las mujeres violadas, los sexos esparcidos y las tripas sacadas,' forgetting that 'la novella no estaba en los muertos … sino en los vivos que debieron sudar hielo en su escondite.' He preferred the indirect mode of Camus' *La Peste* in which the horror is in the atmosphere men breathe and through which they move and not in piles of corpses" (126).

Marxist demand for social realism and defends symbolism. After a vicious civil war, he explains, the Colombian public asked its writers, "When are you going to write something about the violence?"[31] García Márquez begins his answer by discussing the difficulties of describing "the nightmare of violence" (649). The public might assume that witnesses would provide the best accounts, but survivors are not likely to have the literary skill to convey their ordeal to anyone else (647). Even professional writers who attempt to represent violence realistically fail because they produce bad novels. An inventory of crimes is not a work of art:

> The exhaustive inventory of decapitations, castrations, rapes, brains and guts ripped open, the minute description of cruelty with which those crimes were committed, were probably not the way to a novel. The drama was the atmosphere of terror that caused those crimes. (648)

Novels should deal with the living, not the dead; it is the living who had to "sweat ice in their hiding places" (648). Fiction requires a dramatic conflict, he explains, "Because no human drama can be completely unilateral" (650). Serious novelists must remember that "the drama of that period was not only that of the persecuted, but also that of the persecutor" (650). He illustrates these points with Albert Camus's La peste, which was published in 1947. Camus represents the Nazi occupation of France indirectly by imagining the effects of a medieval plague (649). Instead of describing the historical

---

[31] García Márquez, "Dos o tres cosas," 646. My translation.

events of his own time, Camus examines the ambiguity of behavior in extreme circumstances long ago. The parallel between the two periods is implicit; without making comparative judgments, Camus assumes that there are constants in both situations. García Márquez perceives yet another parallel in the violence in Colombia. In 1967, he implemented the insights of his essay in *One Hundred Years of Solitude*, using fantasy to "write something about the violence."

Since extremity, excess, and irony are relative qualities, it seems to be easier for Western readers to recognize them in *Ulysses*, *Berlin Alexanderplatz*, and *The Tin Drum* than in postcolonial texts. The line of influence I am tracing, however, may help readers perceive these qualities in unfamiliar settings. Postcolonial writers convey the multiple meanings of massacres by using irony to discredit the rhetoric that justified them and by making the horror of historical events more incredible than magic. Instead of mixing discourses for ironic effect, in *One Hundred Years of Solitude* García Márquez uses the same tone and even the same vocabulary for empirical reality and fantasy. Words like "prodigious," "fantastic," "miraculous," and "marvelous" recur for both kinds of experience. The disparity between a consistent narrative tone and radically dissimilar events produces formal irony. For example, the narrator describes the massacre of banana workers, a scene based on the Colombian army's retaliation for a strike against the United Fruit Company in 1928, as a magical event:

> After his shout something happened that did not bring on fright but a kind of hallucination. The captain gave the order to fire and fourteen machine guns answered at once. But it all seemed like a farce. It was as if the machine guns had been loaded with caps,

because their panting rattle could be heard and their incandescent spitting could be seen, but not the slightest reaction was perceived, not a cry, not even a sigh among the compact crowd that seemed petrified by an instantaneous invulnerability. Suddenly, on one side of the station, a cry of death tore open the enchantment: "Aaaagh, Mother."[32]

The workers' resistance transcends ordinary experience, at least for a moment. José Arcadio Segunda survives the shooting and attempts to report what happened, but no one believes him. The first woman he tells replies, "'There haven't been any dead here,' she said. 'Since the time of your uncle, the colonel, nothing has happened in Macondo'" (331). José Arcadio Segundo's testimony comes to seem "a hallucinated version, because it was radically opposed to the false one that historians had created and consecrated in the schoolbooks" (375). In contrast to the community's denial, nature avenges the massacre. Rains of biblical duration destroy the banana trees, driving the foreign company away. Despite the symbolic extremity of the downpour, the narrator measures the rain with empirical precision: "It rained for four years, eleven months, and two days" (339). Reversing the conventions of fact and fantasy, the text locates the historical event in a field of competing meanings.

Like García Márquez, Rushdie contradicts readers' expectations to show that human brutality is more incredible than supernatural events. In *Midnight's Children* Saleem's magical powers are treated as

---

[32] Gabriel García Márquez, *One Hundred Years of Solitude*, trans. Gregory Rabassa (New York: Perennial Classics, 1970), 328.

ordinary qualities, but political violence is unbelievable. As Saleem says of the Pakistani army's bombing of civilians, "it was not true because it could not have been true."[33] Instead of attempting to convey the horror of the Amritsar massacre directly, Saleem records it as an event in his grandparents' marriage. Before the massacre, Saleem's grandfather, a physician trained in Germany, tries to help victims of rioting, disinfecting wounds with mercurochrome. When he returns home, his traditional wife thinks the mercurochrome stains on his clothing are blood. Once she realizes that he is not wounded, she is humiliated at her mistake: "'You do it on purpose,' she says, 'to make me look stupid. I am not stupid. I have read several books'" (33). A few days later, British soldiers fire on the unarmed crowd. Fifty soldiers are responsible for more than fifteen hundred civilian casualties, and the commanding officer tells his men, "We have done a jolly good thing" (34). This time Dr. Aziz returns home covered in blood, but his wife calmly assumes the stains are mercurochrome. Focusing on a domestic misunderstanding, Rushdie takes an oblique approach to the enormity of the massacre.

Just as readers' beliefs about the value of love, socialism, and art can muffle the irony of Joyce, Döblin, and Grass, assumptions about unfamiliar cultures can lead to regionalist readings of postcolonial magic realism. And just as Bloom's ascension at the end of the "Cyclops" episode in *Ulysses* and Biberkopf's conversion at the end of *Berlin Alexanderplatz* parody elements of the Judeo-Christian tradition, postcolonial magic realists also use native beliefs ironically as a source of symbolism. Nevertheless, critics influenced by the

---

[33] Rushdie, *Midnight's Children*, 432.

Americanist paradigm interpret the same strategies differently. For example, although the numerous similarities of style and substance in *The Tin Drum* and *Midnight's Children* are widely recognized, Rushdie's symbolic use of fantasy is often interpreted as a realistic representation of India.[34] As Neil ten Kortenaar observes, the "common reading of *Midnight's Children*...regards the magic in magic realism as indigenous...and the realism as Western," reinforcing a "'stereotypical polarity' between Indian spirituality and European worldliness."[35] Similarly, Liam Connell argues that there is a kind of critic who can "define Magic Realism as a culturally specific project, by identifying for his readers those (non-modern) societies where myth and magic persist and where Magic Realism might be expected to occur."[36] Challenging critics who conflate the non-Western and the pre-modern, Connell points out that Joyce's historical situation was similar to that of postcolonial writers: "To distinguish Magic Realism as the product of an oppressive social environment is to ignore the similar impact of Western society on its cultural production. For example, it is immensely significant that Joyce was writing during the period of Irish Independence

---

[34] For detailed comparisons, see Rudolf Bader, "Indian Tin Drum," *International Fiction Review* 11 (1984), 75–83; E. W. Herd, "Tin Drum and Snake-Charmer's Flute: Salman Rushdie's Debt to Günter Grass," *New Comparison* 6 (1988): 205–18; Kenneth R. Ireland, "Doing Very Dangerous Things: *Die Blechtrommel* and *Midnight's Children*," *Comparative Literature* 42 (1990): 335–62; Patricia Merivale, "Saleem Fathered by Oskar: *Midnight's Children*, Magic Realism, and *The Tin Drum*," in *Magical Realism: Theory, History, Community*, ed. Lois Parkinson Zamora and Wendy B. Faris (Durham and London: Duke University Press, 1995), 329–45.

[35] Neil ten Kortenaar, "Salman Rushdie's Magic Realism and the Return of Inescapable Romance," *University of Toronto Quarterly* 71 (2002): 766.

[36] Liam Connell, "Discarding Magic Realism: Modernism, Anthropology, and Critical Practice," *ARIEL* 29 (1998): 102.

and against the dominance of English culture in Ireland" (100–01). Connell warns, "It is important also to be vigilant against making the mistake of thinking that just because García Márquez is Colombian, he believes in the myths that he uses" (107). Critics may be less likely to make this mistake if they recognize that irony is a fundamental characteristic of magic realism.

The magic in postcolonial texts is not necessarily evidence of indigenous belief in supernatural forces. García Márquez and Rushdie, like Döblin and Grass, adapt religious beliefs, recasting their sources into new narratives. Traditional beliefs are not treated as sacred authority or unifying communal ideals. Supernatural events are represented as ordinary, empirical occurrences, not as miracles, and ordinary things acquire nonempirical meanings. Whatever characters in *One Hundred Years of Solitude* or *Midnight's Children* may believe, irony prevents their beliefs from controlling the meaning of the text. In *One Hundred Years of Solitude*, the itinerant gypsy who brings news of the outside world to Macondo says, "Things have a life of their own.... It's simply a matter of waking up their souls."[37] Such a passage might suggest a credulity that fits the Americanist version of magic realism, but the gypsy is describing magnetism, not animism. His words recall Roh's observation that magic realism portrays the spirit in things. Similarly, Remedios the Beauty levitates above the earth, but she ascends on bedsheets that she was told to fold (255). In *Midnight's Children*, Saleem escapes from Pakistan in a magician's "basket of invisibility," but the magician is a communist who "disbelieved ... in the possibility of magic" and "denied the

---

[37] García Márquez, *One Hundred Years of Solitude*, 2.

supernatural."[38] Supernatural events are as symbolic in Colombia and India as they are in Ireland and Germany.

Grass and postcolonial magic realists make the indeterminacy of their texts explicit. Describing incredible events, whether in fantasy or history, they propose multiple, sometimes contradictory, meanings without demanding that readers accept them. As Oskar says of one version of events, it "was true, as we well know, and yet the whole was false."[39] His characteristic attitude is "I still believe and doubt to this day" (119). In *One Hundred Years of Solitude*, García Márquez writes that "no one knew for certain where the limits of reality lay. It was an intricate stew of truths and mirages...."[40] Similarly, Saleem, the first-person narrator of *Midnight's Children*, says, "So—believe me, don't believe, but this is what it was like!"[41] This indeterminacy is Joyce's legacy. At the end of the century, *Midnight's Children* echoes Eliot's praise for the "shape and significance," the "order and form," of *Ulysses*,[42] when Saleem calls on art to take the raw material of life and give it "shape and form—that is to say, meaning."[43] Instead of embracing postcolonial magic realism for its putative transcendence, we can respect the ongoing struggle to give shape and form to historical events.

The common strategies in twentieth-century texts reflect the continuing need to represent unimaginable violence in the absence of communal belief—religious or secular. The First World War, the

---

[38] Rushdie, *Midnight's Children*, 444–45.
[39] Grass, *The Tin Drum*, 73.
[40] García Márquez, *One Hundred Years of Solitude*, 242.
[41] Rushdie, *Midnight's Children*, 409.
[42] Eliot, "*Ulysses*, Order, and Myth," 177 and 178.
[43] Rushdie, *Midnight's Children,* 531.

Second World War, the massacre of banana plantation workers in Colombia, and the Amritsar attack on unarmed civilians were beyond comprehension. Explanations, justifications, and condemnations were inadequate. The challenge of representing these events was to convey their gravity without presuming to define their significance. Joyce showed other writers a way out of this dilemma. The blend of realism and symbolism; the extremity of transgressing formal and social conventions; the excess of people, places, and things; and the ironic disparities in *Ulysses* proved to be useful strategies for other writers. The lesson of *Ulysses* is that when history is a nightmare, realism is both inadequate and indispensable.

6

How to write about the Holocaust

The post-Holocaust commandment "Never forget!" is easy to endorse but hard to obey. The question of how to document and remember the Nazi genocide is urgently debated. As Theodor Adorno warns, "To write poetry after Auschwitz is barbaric."[1] Although the meaning of this statement is disputed, it has acquired the cultural force of an aphorism. It stands as a disavowal of any attempt to represent atrocity.[2] Nevertheless, survivors and many others have felt compelled to speak out. They have produced realist and antirealist representations of genocide, though critics in the field of Holocaust Studies have exposed the weaknesses of both approaches.[3] Realist narratives imply that the unfathomable horror of events is knowable and describable, and antirealist accounts bury the specificity of

---

[1] Adorno, "Cultural Criticism and Society," 34.

[2] See Klaus Hofmann, "Poetry After Auschwitz—Adorno's Dictum," *German Life and Letters* 58 (2005): 183. After detailing the erroneous interpretations of Adorno's statement, Hofmann concedes, "The question whether and how a poem can possibly be written after Auschwitz persists and it pervades Adorno's writing."

[3] See Rothberg, *Traumatic Realism*, 9: "At the center of this book stands the concept of traumatic realism, a concept I derive from Holocaust testimonial writing, but that also has implications for postwar cultural theory. By focusing attention on the intersection of the

events in a "discourse of unrepresentability and unknowability."[4] But if the Holocaust and other atrocities are truly beyond representation, how can they be remembered? Silence may be a form of protest, but it also allows people to forget the past.

W. G. Sebald ponders this impasse in *The Natural History of Destruction*. Appalled by the violence of the Second World War, he writes as a German confronting his country's recent past. He calls attention to the paucity of novels about the German experience of the war and attributes this lack not to guilt but to the same difficulty that victims of the Nazis faced:

> The reality of total destruction, incomprehensible in its extremity, pales when described in such stereotypical phrases as "a prey to the flames," "that fateful night," "all hell was let loose," "we were staring into the inferno," "the dreadful fate of the cities of Germany," and so on and so forth. Their function is to cover up and neutralize experiences beyond our ability to comprehend.[5]

everyday and the extreme in the experience and writing of Holocaust survivors, traumatic realism provides an aesthetic and cognitive solution to the conflicting demands inherent in representing and understanding genocide. Traumatic realism mediates between the realist and antirealist positions in Holocaust studies and marks the necessity of considering how the ordinary and extraordinary aspects of genocide intersect and coexist." See also Jenni Adams, *Magic Realism in Holocaust Literature: Troping the Traumatic Real* (Hampshire: Palgrave Macmillan, 2011), 24–29. Adams uses Rothberg's distinction between realist and antirealist approaches in her discussion of the "necessity/difficulty opposition" in theories about representing the Holocaust (23). She associates "traumatic realism" with magic realism (29). By combining realism and antirealism, magic realist narratives offer a third alternative: "Knowledge of the Holocaust may thus be understood in the sense not only of a factual acquaintance with the event but also of an adequate grasp of both its magnitude and its traumatic experiential impact" (24).

[4] Adams, *Magic Realism in Holocaust Literature*, 28.
[5] Sebald, *On the Natural History of Destruction*, 24–25.

When descriptions of extremity are not extreme, eyewitness accounts fail to convey what victims experienced: "The apparently unimpaired ability—shown in most of the eyewitness reports—of everyday language to go on functioning as usual raises doubts of the authenticity of the experiences they record" (25). Furthermore, since any eyewitness account is only one person's experience, it cannot convey the enormity of an event. Sebald proposes an alternative: "The accounts of individual eyewitnesses, therefore, are of only qualified value, and need to be supplemented by what a synoptic and artificial view reveals" (25–26). A "synoptic" view is more comprehensive than any witness's perspective. While such a view is "artificial" in its scope, Sebald seems to be endorsing more radical kinds of distortion. Taken with his critique of everyday language, his call for a "synoptic and artificial view" implies a willingness to sacrifice accuracy and authenticity for rhetorical impact.[6] Much of the critical debate about how to remember the Holocaust pits eyewitness testimony against aesthetic invention, yet these alternatives are too schematic for narratives that are neither realist nor antirealist. The continuing need to represent unimaginable violence is both illustrated and theorized in two interconnected texts about the Second World War: Sebald's *Austerlitz* and H. G. Adler's *Panorama*. Like Günter Grass, both authors combine realism and antirealism, only to jettison both forms of narrative in favor of physical evidence.

---

[6] See Todd Samuel Presner, "'What a Synoptic and Artificial View Reveals': Extreme History and the Modernism of W. G. Sebald's Realism," *Criticism* 46 (2004): 356–57. Presner interprets a "synoptic and artificial" view as one achieved through "the multiplicity and simultaneity of its many contingent perspectives," which is "utterly 'artificial,' because no eyewitness could have possibly seen it as described. It is an imaginary, artificially constructed view of a real historical event."

Dissatisfied with the modernist method of tethering meanings to the objective world, Sebald and Adler also reject the magic realist method of mixing fact and fantasy. Instead, they foreground the empirical meaning of things. In addition to using objects symbolically, they speak of things as if they had agency. In *The Tin Drum*, Oskar says that wallpaper has a better memory than people do; in *Austerlitz* and *Panorama*, the detritus of people's lives provides evidence of their existence, even if no one remembers them. This devolution from human memory to matter appears less dire in the context of new materialist theories, particularly those of Bruno Latour and Bill Brown.[7] These theorists attribute agency, an agency comparable to our own, to the material world. Latour refers to all agents as "actants" in a network of relations.[8] Brown conceptualizes the capacity of objects to bear meaning apart from human intentions as the "social life of things."[9] He explains that thing theory rejects the "ontological distinction, arbitrary and artificial, between inanimate

---

[7] Maurizia Boscagli, *Stuff Theory: Everyday Objects, Radical Materialism* (New York: Bloomsbury Academic, 2014), 3. Boscagli argues that the "rubric of the 'new materialisms'" encompasses the "'thing theory' of Bill Brown" as well as Bruno Latour's "notion of the quasi-subject quasi-object—that is, [a]… (dis)order of things in which friable subjects and mutable objects intervene in each others' [sic] being," a notion that "may be the pivotal idea of the new materialism."

[8] Bruno Latour, "On actor-network theory. A few clarifications plus more than a few complications," *Soziale Welt* 47 (1996): 369–81. http://www.bruno-latour.fr/sites/default/files/P-67%20ACTOR-NETWORK.pdf, 7. Actant "implies *no* special motivation of *human individual* actors, nor of humans in general. An actant can literally be anything provided it is granted to be the source of an action."

[9] Bill Brown, "Thing Theory," *Critical Inquiry* 28 (2001): 6. Brown further distinguishes things from the more general category of objects. Positing the "all-at-onceness, the simultaneity, of the object/thing dialectic," he explains, "You could imagine things… as what is excessive in objects, as what exceeds their mere materialization as objects or their mere utilization as objects" (5).

objects and human subjects."[10] Latour and Brown affirm the rights of all actants and challenge the ethical legitimacy of prioritizing human interests. These claims surpass Franz Roh's description of the bond between the "forms of the spirit and the very solidity of objects" in magic realism.[11] While magic realists perceive meaning in objects, new materialists discern not only meaning but agency in objects. The agency of things may be metaphorical in art or literature, but new materialists consider matter a real force in the world. Abandoning the fundamental divide between animate and inanimate entities, new materialists emphasize the impact of matter on our lives. Although they attribute agency to actants that are incapable of intention, they do not distribute responsibility throughout the network. All actants may have agency and rights, but only humans can be held accountable for their actions. While new materialists want to expand the ethical universe beyond anthropocentric interests, the meaning of things in *Panorama* and *Austerlitz* registers rhetorical despair. These texts treat objects as more reliable agents than people are.

Eliminating the binary of mutable matter and immutable mind or spirit does not indicate that matter is a new foundation of meaning. Brown warns against elevating matter to the permanence once attributed to spirit: "Objects cannot be depended on as a source of continuity in the midst of human flux because objects, too, are mutable. They too have lives (and deaths) of their own."[12] To clarify the difference between things and symbols, Brown cites precursors

---

[10] Bill Brown, *A Sense of Things: The Object Matter of American Literature* (Chicago: University of Chicago Press, 2003), 187.

[11] Faris, "Magical Realism," 22.

[12] Brown, *A Sense of Things*, 183.

of the new materialisms. He points out that twentieth-century poets such as Marianne Moore and William Carlos Williams "aggressively tried to avoid making physical objects symbolic" (171). The poets' aesthetic discipline, Brown argues, overcame our common longing "for there to be some physical object with which, or through which, we can organize and stabilize knowledge and power, human emotion and human history" (171). If, as Williams proclaimed, "there are 'no ideas but in things'" (171), things acquire the epistemological status of evidence rather than symbols. Although *evidence* is not a term that new materialists use, it is a more familiar way to describe the capacity of objects to contain meanings without becoming symbols or metonyms that stand for something else. For example, a gun is an inert object, but if it is used in a homicide, it enters a network of meanings as the murder weapon. Similarly, like Grass, Sebald and Adler construct narratives about things that establish their specific connections to events.

Sebald would object to being compared to Grass. Surveying postwar German novels in *The Natural History of Destruction*, Sebald omits *The Tin Drum*, possibly because he had already criticized Grass in "Constructs of Mourning: Günter Grass and Wolfgang Hildesheimer" (1983). Focusing on *From the Diary of a Snail*, this essay faults Grass for failing to imagine the experience of the Jews of Danzig. Sebald regards Grass's use of Erwin Lichtenstein's historical study "The Exodus of the Jews from the Free City of Danzig" as a sign that "German *literati* still know little of the real fate of the persecuted Jews."[13] Grass's inability to imagine the impact of the war on its

---

[13] W. G. Sebald, "Constructs of Mourning: Günter Grass and Wolfgang Hildesheimer," in *Campo Santo*, trans. Anthea Bell, ed. Sven Meyer (London: Penguin, 2006), 113.

victims, Sebald claims, "shows that literature today, left solely to its own devices, is no longer able to discover the truth" (114).[14] Grass's dependence on "documentary material" corroborates his "wishful thinking" that "there really were Germans of a better kind" (115). As an artist, Grass should have identified with victims.

Defending Grass, Peter Morgan presents the argument for eyewitness testimony in "'Your Story is now My Story': The Ethics of Narration in Grass and Sebald." Morgan weighs the narratives of the two authors on moral and ethical scales, distinguishing the moral authority of memory from the ethical responsibility of history. Reversing Sebald's critique of Grass for "failing *to tell the stories of* the Danzig Jews," Morgan argues that in *Austerlitz* Sebald's attempt to imagine what Jews experienced is unethical.[15] Adhering to the principle that only victims can know what was done to them, Morgan claims that Sebald "cannot be a moral witness" because he did not experience the events he writes about (199). Understanding Sebald's aim as "invention of the truth" rather than "discovery of the truth" (203, n. 22), Morgan censures him for usurping the moral authority of witnesses and presuming to speak for the victim rather than the persecutor (199). Applying the standard of "historical specificity and clarity in remembering" (198), Morgan objects to Sebald's method of merging "self and other, past and present, victim and perpetrator, memory and history" (199):

---

[14] Peter Morgan, "'Your Story is now My Story': The Ethics of Narration in Grass and Sebald," *Monatshefte* 101 (2009): 203, n. 22. Morgan corrects Anthea Bell's translation, arguing that the last phrase should be "to invent the truth," because Sebald's point "depends on the distinction between" the terms for "invention of the truth" and "discovery of the truth."
[15] Morgan, "Ethics of Narration," 189.

Where Grass distinguishes voices and refrains from speaking for the other, Sebald's narrative voice remains the same regardless of whose story he is retelling, be it his own or that of his interlocutors. His writing style reduces everything to the same undifferentiated tenor of universal suffering, blotting out distinctions of history, place and identity. (196)

Morgan blames the uniformity of Sebald's voice for conflating the suffering of Germans and Jews during the war (199). If everyone sounds the same, no one can be held responsible. Whereas Sebald worries that witnesses' accounts trivialize destruction, Morgan grants victims unique moral authority.

Despite the stark opposition in the polemic, Grass imagines Jewish characters in *The Tin Drum*, and Sebald cites Jewish sources in *Austerlitz*. Notwithstanding Sebald's low opinion of Grass's imagination, Grass not only creates Jewish characters but also invents the truth. For example, in *The Tin Drum*, the toy merchant Sigismund Markus is a victim of *Kristallnacht*, and Herr Fajngold is the sole survivor of a family "put in the ovens at Treblinka."[16] Like Sebald, Grass dreads falling into clichés. In his memoir *Peeling the Onion*, Grass describes the difficulty of expressing his own experience of the war; he has read too many war stories based on other war stories. The combination of realism and fantasy in *The Tin Drum* is an extreme instance of a "synoptic and artificial" view of the war. Grass's irony is quite unlike Sebald's earnestness, yet *The Tin Drum* also responds to the need to bear witness to violence.

---

[16] Grass, *The Tin Drum*, 380.

Furthermore, Sebald uses documentary material too. *Austerlitz*, as Morgan points out, is indebted to H. G. Adler's *Theresienstadt* (1955), a survivor's description of the concentration camp outside Prague. Austerlitz reads this "heavy tome, running to almost eight hundred close-printed pages" and regrets "that now it is too late for me to seek out Adler."[17] This comment suggests that the narrator considers the documentary record inadequate. Perhaps Austerlitz expects additional insights from a "flesh-witness." This is Yuval Noah Harari's term based on a French soldier's statement that a man "who has not understood *with his flesh* cannot talk to you about it."[18] Harari contrasts the empirical knowledge of the eyewitness with the inner knowledge of the participant, who believes, "You had to undergo the experience yourself in order to understand it."[19] The experience is valued for what it reveals. Harari connects this conviction to the "aesthetics and epistemology of the sublime" (281). As he explains, the Kantian sublime has two stages:

In the first stage, encounters with the sublime experiences of war overwhelm the combatant and disillusion him about many of his peacetime ideas and ideals. Yet by releasing the combatant from his peacetime illusions these experiences make room for a better and more authentic perception of reality. The combatant then enjoys various positive revelations, which more than compensate

---

[17] W. G. Sebald, *Austerlitz*, trans. Anthea Bell (New York: Modern Library, 2001), 232 and 236. Sebald says that Adler wrote *Theresienstadt* from 1945 to 1947, though it was not published until 1955 (233).
[18] Harari, "Scholars, Eyewitnesses, and Flesh-Witnesses of War," 215.
[19] Harari, *Ultimate Experience*, 232.

for his initial disappointment, particularly because these new revelations bear the authenticating mark of reality. (281)

Despite the terror of the sublime, it is a source of meaning. The revelation itself is not positive, but it becomes the bedrock of truth for the flesh-witness.

Having been in Theresienstadt, Auschwitz, and Buchenwald,[20] Adler unquestionably had the authority of the flesh-witness. A few months after being liberated, he spoke of his experience as the kind of sublime epiphany that Harari finds in soldiers' memoirs. In a letter to a friend, he wrote: "I have experienced terrible things, but since I have experienced them, I don't regret it, and would not be without it."[21] Jeremy Adler recalls: "My father used to say that he learned more in the fortnight he spent in Auschwitz than anywhere else in his life" (34). But unlike most victims, who feel that their experience is indescribable, Adler was determined to record the violence he witnessed. In an interview in 1986, he reconstructed his thoughts:

I will not survive this. But if I survive, then I will describe it, and through two different means: I will research it in scholarly manner and in such form leave myself completely out of it, and I will also describe it in a poetic manner. I have done both, and the fact that I have done so does not mean all that much, but it is a small justification for my having survived. The transformation of

---

[20] Jeremy Adler, "The World of My Father's Memory Writing: The *Gesamtkunstwerk* of H. G. Adler," in *H. G. Adler: Life, Literature, Legacy*, ed. Julia Creet, Sara R. Horowitz, and Amira Bojadzija-Dan (Evanston, IL: Northwestern University Press, 2016), 25.
[21] Quoted in Jeremy Adler, "World of My Father's Memory Writing," 25–26.

this experience into literary works provided me with unbelievable strength ... Yes, it was an act of liberation.[22]

Theresienstadt was written in a "scholarly manner," and it fulfilled part of his intention: "Whoever takes the trouble to read the apporximately 1,000 pages, will really have been in the camp."[23] Having described the *what*, he turned to the *why* in a trilogy of novels beginning with *Panorama*. Although *Panorama* was not published until 1968 and not translated into English until 2011, it was completed in 1948. Adler's conviction that art had sustained him counters Adorno's prohibition of art after Auschwitz. If Sebald had, in fact, met Adler, they would have agreed on the benefits of a "synoptic and artificial view" of destruction. While Adler speaks with the moral authority of a witness as Morgan demands, he also invents the truth of a novelist as Sebald requires.

To convey the experiential knowledge of a flesh-witness, Adler adopted modernist techniques. Jeremy Adler comments, "Adler sought a path characterized by its complexity and, indeed, its *difficulty*. Difficulty is a distinctly modernist characteristic—one recalls Stéphane Mallarmé and Paul Celan—and by adopting difficulty as a response to the Shoah in his scholarship and above all in his fiction, H. G. Adler can be said to have used the appropriate mode with which to approach the modernist cataclysm" (27). In contrast to his eyewitness report in *Theresienstadt*, Adler does not rely on factual testimony in

---

[22] Quoted in Peter Filkins, "The Self Positioned, the (De)posited Self, the Soul Released: The Uses of Biography in H. G. Adler's Shoah Trilogy," in *H. G. Adler: Life, Literature, Legacy*, ed. Julia Creet, Sara R. Horowitz, and Amira Bojadzija-Dan (Evanston, IL: Northwestern University Press, 2016), 47.

[23] Quoted in Jeremy Adler, "World of My Father's Memory Writing," 30–31.

Panorama. He writes in a "poetic manner," and *Panorama* shows the influence of modernist writers. In the translator's introduction, Peter Filkins points out that the protagonist's name, Josef Kramer, alludes to Kafka's *The Trial* and that the narrative point of view resembles Joyce's stream-of-consciousness technique in *A Portrait of the Artist as a Young Man*.[24] In addition, *Panorama*, like *Portrait*, consists of a series of episodes in the protagonist's life. Adler dwells on key points in Josef's development from childhood in Prague during the First World War to adulthood. The narrative is focalized through Josef, and the free indirect style of each episode reflects his age at the time. As the title suggests, however, the emphasis is on the world he observes. In an "Afterword" to the novel, Peter Demetz marvels at "the abundance and density of details."[25] For example, conducting a room-by-room tour of his boarding school, Josef explains the need for a padlock or even "a combination lock, which you have to know which way to turn in order to open."[26] Instructions for opening a combination lock are important to a young boy, if not to most readers. Such details are excruciating, both because no one wants so much information and because everything Josef notices has been destroyed.

As in *Ulysses*, the excessive amount of information accommodates innumerable patterns of meaning. For example, the opening scene

[24] Peter Filkins, "Introduction," *Panorama*, by H. G. Adler, trans. Peter Filkins (New York: Random House, 2011), xii and xv. See also Omer Bartov, "H. G. Adler and First-Person History," in *H. G. Adler: Life, Literature, Legacy*, ed. Julia Creet, Sara R. Horowitz, and Amira Bojadzija-Dan (Evanston, IL: Northwestern University Press, 2016), 119–20. Bartov notes: "That the notorious Nazi perpetrator and the last commandant of the Bergen-Belsen concentration camp, Josef Kramer, shares the name of *Panorama*'s main character, may be either coincidence or intentional."
[25] Peter Demetz, "Afterword," in *Panorama*, by H. G. Adler, trans. Peter Filkins (New York: Random House, 2011, 449.
[26] H. G. Adler, *Panorama*, trans. Peter Filkins (New York: Random House, 2011), 107.

establishes a specific meaning for *panorama* as a small theater where illuminated slides are viewed through peepholes, yet as the word recurs, it acquires symbolic resonance. Comparing *Panorama* to *Austerlitz*, Filkins notes that both texts "seem to be carefully researched factual studies of the author's own experience, replete with their own panorama of photographs, but which are also highly manipulated forays into the fictional sublime."[27] Symbolic meanings that transcend empirical description evoke the "sublime." Adler's combination of the factual and the fictional, and the realistic and the symbolic, provides the "synoptic and artificial view" that Sebald advocates. The factual parts of *Panorama* represent events and experiences, and the "fictional sublime" conveys their many meanings.

While the text combines realism and symbolism, Josef voices a wariness of symbols that resembles Oskar's refusal to accept a substitute for his drum. For example, on a camping trip with the Wanderers, a youth club dedicated to appreciating nature, someone suggests making a flag, but Josef protests the use of a symbol to unify the group: "If the Wanderers really want to be entirely natural, then they have to abstain from using any outward symbols."[28] The leader of the group disagrees, arguing that "everything in the world is symbolic, and if you employ a symbol in a disingenuous manner, then it means nothing, for you have to distinguish between a symbol and an allegory" (146). In contrast, Josef's best friend in the group demonstrates a better way to make the Wanderers' activities meaningful. He proposes historical and literary parallels to the

---

[27] Filkins, "Introduction," xix.
[28] Adler, *Panorama*, 146.

present, a strategy that fits Eliot's definition of the mythical method. Josef admiringly remarks, "[He] is never caught off guard, and always has examples from Homer or history at hand when the others howl and complain" (156). In the final episode, Josef reviews the events of his life as if they were scenes in the panorama of his childhood, changing them when "a little bell rings" (406), until he stops himself: "But what did you once say about symbols?" (407). His question highlights the difference between symbols, which substitute one thing for another, and parallels, which identify constants among discrete entities. Unlike symbols, parallels preserve the distinctive qualities of each entity, and Adler uses them to align Josef's experience of the war with earlier events.

Turning to the Nazi period only in the final episodes, Adler stages debates on the problem of representing violence. Initially sent to a labor camp, Josef and other prisoners try to make the best of their situation. Josef wants "to have a good understanding of the way things work ... so that he can adapt to them" (317). Dr. Siegler, one of the older men, finds consolation in the "views of philosophers from Heraclitus to Nietzsche," claiming "that he may indeed be a victim, but he is also a witness" (343). He has a "freedom, namely the freedom of knowledge or the ability to know" (344). He advises the younger men to think about better times, because "memory is solace" (344). Josef understands Siegler's reasoning: "Whoever does not hold such a world within himself, whoever can't save it, he is today lost before he is even killed, for all will be killed, but Siegler hopes for the strength to maintain such solace right up until that last horrible moment" (345). Josef disagrees. He distrusts "any grand theory, for what we can know is a present, namely *the* present.... In this sense memory is of no use" (350). Eventually, Josef is transferred to Auschwitz-Birkenau, and there he finds that thinking about the present is equally useless. Here "knowledge and culture have become pointless," and language has become "incapable of expressing the nature of the lost in a way that would be comprehensible to those on the outside" (355). Like Marlow in *Heart of Darkness*, like the soldiers Harari studies, Josef believes his experiences are inexpressible.

Nevertheless, just as Marlow proposes a parallel to colonialism in the Roman occupation of Britain, Josef turns to the historical past for a parallel to understand his experience. After he is released from Langenstein Camp (a division of Buchenwald), he goes to Cornwall and visits Launceston Castle, which was built by William the Conqueror. In addition to the coincidental echo of place names, a plaque points out an earlier instance of religious persecution. Oliver Cromwell imprisoned the Quaker George Fox in the dungeon of Launceston. The parallel gives Josef space to think about his torment at the behest of the German "Conqueror" (406). The similarities between conquerors in England and Germany remind Josef that people are already turning "away from the horror of yesterday's atrocities" (410). In the peace of the park at Launceston Castle, Josef confronts the question of life, not art, after Auschwitz. He asks, "For how is it that one comes to survive his own destruction?" (410). His problem is not how to remember but how to forget. To obey the imperative, "Never forget," would prolong his suffering, and he welcomes the "power of forgetfulness" (410). As Jeremy Adler, writing about his father's work, observes, "And then, memory condemns the victims to everlasting subjugation—a central, but largely unreflected aporia of our collective remembrance."[29] It may be more important for witnesses to forget than to remember.

In his disordered mental state, Josef is not "sure any longer whether he is someone who has acted or is a witness or a victim, or whether he is all of these together in having been part of history or if he simply overheard a bunch of tales."[30] His own experiences seem unreal to him. He thinks of himself as an object rather than a subject: "Most likely a person exists only by virtue of the world that is mirrored within him. Josef is an object of the world, so any hope of engaging with it is an idle thought" (427). He is not just dehumanized, not just objectified; he is less than a thing: "Matter is the victor over essence, which in turn likes to be immortalized as the unvanquished" (431). Josef wants to forget, but matter wants to remember. As in *Austerlitz* and *The Tin Drum*, in *Panorama* matter is a better witness than people are.

Although Sebald and Adler employ testimony and invention, and realism and antirealism, to represent the Holocaust, neither author relies on the testimony of witnesses. Like Grass, Sebald and Adler show that objects bear witness to human acts as evidence, not because they are symbols of anything else. More trustworthy than human memory, feeling, or belief, things are meaningful in their empirical presence apart from any associations projected onto them. The symbol reaches for multiple meanings, but the object is inert. Its simple presence marks a connection to the past. Just as Oskar in *The Tin Drum* says

---

[29] Jeremy Adler, "Good Against Evil? H. G. Adler, T. W. Adorno and the Representation of the Holocaust," in *The German-Jewish Dilemma from the Enlightenment to the Shoah*, ed. Edward Timms and Andrea Hammel (Lewiston: Edwin Mellen Press, 1999), 262.
[30] Adler, *Panorama*, 440.

that "even wallpaper has a better memory than human beings,"[31] Josef concedes that matter is the victor over spirit. Critical debates about who has the right to record the past are beside the point, because *no one* remembers well enough. The inadequacy of testimony causes all three authors to trust matter more than memory.

Sebald's critique of Grass's use of Jewish sources acknowledges an exception to the evasions of *From the Diary of a Snail*:

> One of the passages in the *Diary* where an appearance of truth is created by the confrontation of historical reality and retrospective fiction is a passage about the transports taking those Jewish children who were able to leave Danzig to England.[32]

Sebald makes such transports the kernel of *Austerlitz*.[33] As a child, Austerlitz is evacuated from Prague, not Danzig, and placed with a taciturn Welsh couple, who never tell him that he is adopted. He eventually returns to Prague and learns that his mother was sent to Terezín (Czech for Theresienstadt) and his father fled to Paris. Austerlitz goes to both places seeking information about their last years. Although this summary implies that the characters are conceived as coherent individuals, they are constructed as composites, and the plot is based on coincidence rather than motivation. The text is saturated with meanings, but they are not grounded in psychological consistency or causal relationships. Instead, contingent

---

[31] Grass, *The Tin Drum*, 177.

[32] Sebald, "Constructs of Mourning," 116.

[33] See also Alfred Thomas, *Prague Palimpsest: Writing, Memory, and the City* (Chicago: University of Chicago Press, 2010), 159. Thomas reports that Sebald "first came across the raw material for his novel *Austerlitz* in a Channel 4 television documentary which related the experience of two orphaned Czech Jews who came to England on the *Kindertransport* and were brought up by Welsh Calvinists."

parallels among discrete entities—people, animals, places, events, and things—provide the conditions for endless possibilities of meaning.

This proliferation is usually unified by the psychoanalytic concept of traumatic repression. From a Freudian perspective, Austerlitz's unconscious is the organizing principle for otherwise random associations, causing them to be motivated rather than contingent. Suggesting the pace of analysis, the narrator describes the slow process of becoming acquainted with Austerlitz, who in turn describes the slow process of discovering his own past. Separated from his parents as a child, he stifles his memories of home until he is an adult. His state of neither remembering nor forgetting fits the psychoanalytic definition of repression, a possible response to trauma. In *Unclaimed Experience: Trauma, Narrative, and History*, Cathy Caruth explains trauma as "an experience that is not fully assimilated as it occurs" and therefore takes the form of "repression and repetitive reappearance."[34] Austerlitz displays these symptoms of trauma, which in his case is not due to violence but to being separated from his parents. He erects barriers "against the emergence of memory,"[35] causing "the almost total paralysis of [his] linguistic faculties" (140). Attempting to write about his studies, he confronts "the inadequacy of all the words I had employed" (122). As an adult, he realizes "how hard I must always have tried to recollect as little as possible" (139), and he explains his "accumulation of knowledge ... as a substitute or compensatory memory" (140). Facts about history, architecture, people, and places help him avoid his own memories. Despite these symptoms

---

[34] Caruth, *Unclaimed Experience*, 5 and 20.
[35] Sebald, *Austerlitz*, 214.

of traumatic repression, however, Austerlitz does not consider his inability to remember unusual. He observes that everyone's memory is limited. With each death, the little that a person remembers disappears:

> as I think how little we can hold in mind, how everything is constantly lapsing into oblivion with every extinguished life, how the world is, as it were, draining itself, in that the history of countless places and objects which themselves have no power of memory is never heard, never described or passed on. (24)

Even people who have not suffered traumatic events fail to remember, and Austerlitz regards his loss of memory as an extreme instance of a general human condition.

Although psychoanalytic theory can explain why Austerlitz forgets, it has less to say about how he remembers. Sebald bypasses the therapeutic process of free association and shifts the burden of remembering from people to things. Austerlitz acquires information about the past through empirical observation of the external world. He tells the narrator that one day he entered the waiting room at the Liverpool Street Station "through a series of coincidences," and memories of being there as a child suddenly returned (138). He goes to Prague and again sees the objects he saw as a child. Walking through the city, he feels that "memories were revealing themselves to me not by means of any mental effort but through my senses, so long numbed and now coming back to life" (150). The objects he sees are not symbols; they are remnants of his past that have survived. Unable to trust human memory, Sebald, like Grass and Adler, turns to matter for evidence of the past. In *Austerlitz*, objects and places speak to the characters, bearing witness and commemorating events.

As things become more distinct, people lose their individuality. The composite identities of Sebald's characters are unstable and contingent. Austerlitz recounts his observations and reflections to an unnamed narrator, who absorbs Austerlitz's story so thoroughly that their voices merge. The first time Austerlitz speaks, his words are folded into the narrator's:

> Towards the end of the nineteenth century, Austerlitz began, in reply to my questions about the history of the building of Antwerp station, when Belgium, a little patch of yellowish gray barely visible on the map of the world, spread its sphere of influence to the African continent with its colonial enterprises .... (9)

Austerlitz's accounts of conversations with other people have the same flat tone. Long sentences meander along contingent paths of speculation. Even the photographs in the text blur distinctions among characters. For example, the narrator uses Austerlitz's photographs to illustrate his own visit to the Antwerp Nocturama (7). He juxtaposes a photograph of the eyes of owls with one of Wittgenstein's eyes, showing the "inquiring gaze found in certain painters and philosophers who seek to penetrate the darkness which surrounds us purely by means of looking and thinking" (5). This homogenization of voices and images paradoxically increases the number of possible connections among entities as it diminishes the individuality of each one. Although Morgan condemns this sameness for blurring responsibility, the narrative makes a different ethical point. The characters in *Austerlitz* are assembled like objects.

Alfred Thomas in *Prague Palimpsest* explains how Sebald pieced his characters together. Thomas demonstrates that many parts of Austerlitz's story are taken from the lives of Kafka and Paul Celan.[36] Whereas most "critical studies of the novel seem to take the protagonist's past at face value," Thomas shows "how the novel exposes the secondary, citational function of these memories" (156). He marshals evidence of Sebald's specific sources to contest readings that claim the narrative "represses memories of unspeakable horror by withholding an authentic voice which could give utterance to such recollections" (162). The concept of repression assumes that experiences shape the individual, but composite characters do not fit this model of subjectivity. They lack the psychological development of a subject assumed to possess conscious and unconscious memories. Thomas argues that "this lack of authentic voice can also be explained in terms of Prague as palimpsest. What the city-text ultimately reveals is not so much a repressed set of authentic memories waiting to be uncovered as a curious absence of authentic memory" (162). Characters constructed from fragments of famous people's lives lack the coherence that would make them seem authentic.

Just as Austerlitz's life is a composite of biographical facts, the name "Jacques Austerlitz" is a knot of historical references. In the Battle of Austerlitz, Napoleon defeated the Russo-Austrian alliance at a site that is now part of the Czech Republic. Since Austerlitz is born in Prague, his French and German names connect him to the nineteenth-century

---

[36] Thomas, *Prague Palimpsest*, 159–65. See also Lynn L. Wolff, "H. G. Adler and W. G. Sebald: From History and Literature to Literature as Historiography," *Monatshefte* 103 (2011): 273, n. 58. Wolff points out resemblances to the life of Saul Friedländer, a victim and historian of the Holocaust born in Prague.

war as well as to the Second World War. Lest these connections suggest
that the main character is a symbol of European history, Sebald
adds the coincidental fact that "Austerlitz" is the real name of Fred
Astaire.[37] This true but random fact gives Austerlitz the opportunity to
construct another parallel to his own life. He tells the narrator that the
freight trains Fred Astaire heard as a child in Nebraska instilled a desire
for long railroad journeys, suggesting Austerlitz's own connection
to railway stations as well as the freight cars the Nazis used to carry
prisoners to concentration camps. Another parallel is that the
Battle of Austerlitz is as hard to represent as the Second World War.
Austerlitz recalls his history teacher's frustration at the inadequacy of
description: "All of us, even when we think we have noted every tiny
detail, resort to set pieces," and "we find the pictures that make up the
stock-in-trade of the spectacle of history forcing themselves upon us"
(71). Yet bloodshed is not what matters most: we stare at images of
battle "while the truth lies elsewhere, away from it all, somewhere as
yet undiscovered" (72). Even for historians, the "truth" is beyond the
factual accounts of witnesses.

Sebald's attention to things is one of the ways he seeks the truth
that lies elsewhere. Although Grass and Adler are disheartened
when they say that things are more reliable than people are, Sebald
attributes agency to things with gratitude. Like new materialists
who respect the ethical claims of animate and inanimate agents,
Sebald regards things as powerful sources of meaning. Returning
to one of the railway stations he passed through as a child,
Austerlitz says:

---

[37] Sebald, *Austerlitz*, 68.

the idea, ridiculous in itself, that this cast-iron column, which with its scaly surface seemed almost to approach the nature of a living being, might remember me and was, if I may so put it, said Austerlitz, a witness to what I could no longer recollect for myself. (221)

Things do not interpret, explain, or construct meanings; they are meaningful as evidence. They become "actants," capable of bearing witness. The binaries of animate and inanimate, human and animal, actual and imagined seem to dissolve. Even "the border between life and death," Austerlitz says, "is less impermeable than we commonly think" (283). He pushes the process of remembering outward, from personal associations to sensory perception of the external world. Objects replace the individual subject as the repository of experience.

Sebald's use of photographs reinforces the meaning of things by making the particularity of the empirical world visible in the text. Like the narrative, the photographs can be interpreted from the perspective of psychoanalysis as well as new materialisms.[38] In *The Generation of Postmemory: Writing and Visual Culture After the Holocaust*, Marianne Hirsch argues that the photographs in *Austerlitz* trigger emotions but do not provide information. The images, she writes, "amount to no more than impersonal building

---

[38] See Carolin Duttlinger, "Traumatic Photographs: Remembrance and the Technical Media in W. G. Sebald's *Austerlitz*," in *W. G. Sebald: A Critical Companion*, ed. J. J. Long and Anne Whitehead (Seattle: University of Washington Press, 2004), 163. Duttlinger argues from a psychoanalytic perspective that photography is "crucial for an engagement with repressed traumatic experiences not because it records what is normally excluded from consciousness but because it provides a substitute for these experiences."

blocks of affiliative postmemory."[39] Their meaning is "shaped by the reality of the *viewer's needs and desires* rather than by the subject's actual 'having-been-there'" (48). In her view, each photograph that apparently documents something specific becomes one of "several fictional devices to throw doubt on every element of the plot and to leave readers disoriented" (50). Hirsch concludes that "Austerlitz goes to the picture for information about the past, but all he finds is the affects and emotions associated with it" (50).

Austerlitz's narrative, however, reverses this process. He regards photographs as the source of affects and emotions. His "needs and desires" do not shape the meaning of the photographs; the photographs shape him. Vera, who took care of Austerlitz as a child, shows him a picture of himself costumed as a "child cavalier,"[40] yet it stirs no memories in him. To Vera, however, the old photographs seem alive, "as if the pictures had a memory of their own and remembered us, remembered the roles that we, the survivors, and those no longer among us had played in our former lives" (182–83). Attributing "a memory of their own" to the pictures, she conflates the animate and the inanimate, granting agency to things. She conveys the impact of photographs as agents of meaning rather than passive objects. The photographs are representations, not reflections, of reality, yet their rhetorical effect is to bear witness. Film records something that existed in front of the camera lens, however grainy, selective, or manipulated the image may be. Moreover, Austerlitz regards his photographs as evidence of reality: they are concerned "with the shape and the self-contained nature of discrete things"

---

[39] Marianne Hirsch, *The Generation of Postmemory: Writing and Visual Culture after the Holocaust* (New York: Columbia University Press, 2012), 42.
[40] Sebald, *Austerlitz*, 184.

(76–77). The images in the text emphasize the importance of material reality.

Sebald demonstrates how objects bear witness to the Holocaust when Austerlitz goes to Terezín, the fortress town outside Prague that the Nazis turned into a concentration camp. In 1991, a Ghetto Museum was opened as part of the Terezín Memorial. Austerlitz comes to this place because his mother was imprisoned here, and he feels that a "panorama" opens for him (186). As he wanders the streets, he draws parallels between the "star-shaped town" of Terezín (283), which was built as a fortress (199), and other star-shaped fortresses turned into prisons: "And whenever I think of the museum in Terezín now, said Austerlitz, I see the framed ground plan of the star-shaped fortifications" of Breendonk (199). The Breendonk fortress, as the narrator explains, was built to protect Antwerp, but the Germans captured it in the First World War and used it as a penal camp until 1944 (19). Coincidentally, the summer residence of Archduke Ferdinand was star shaped (252), and his assassins were imprisoned in Terezín. Austerlitz's awareness of various star-shaped buildings in distant places creates a pattern of fortifications that can protect or imprison. The pattern is a necessary condition for meaning but does not impose any.

Austerlitz documents his visit to Terezín with photographs, though he calls attention to the ambiguity of photography. He locates a copy of the propaganda film that the Germans made in preparation for the Red Cross inspection of Terezín in 1944.[41] He knows that the film deliberately falsifies the prisoners' daily lives,

---

[41] See Jeremy Adler, "Good Against Evil," 279. Jeremy Adler mentions this film in his account of his father's correspondence with Adorno. After H. G. Adler gave the Loeb Lecture in Frankfurt in 1956 on "Theresienstadt: The Lessons of a Concentration Camp,"

yet he pores over each frame hoping to find information about his mother. Viewing the film in slow motion, he sees "previously hidden objects and people, creating, by default as it were, a different sort of film altogether."[42] The film records actual people in a particular place and time, yet the images yield antithetical meanings. The images are authentic, but their meaning is not transparent. The photographs are neither artificial, as critics like Hirsch suggest, nor reliable. They are representations, and their meaning depends on how they are interpreted. Similarly, the photographs of Terezín in *Austerlitz* document it not as it appeared in 1944 or in the 1960s when the narrator meets Austerlitz but recently enough for the images to be reproduced by Rick Poynor in 2004 for a blog about Sebald.[43] Austerlitz is a fictitious character, but the photographs show that Terezín is real.

Walking through the town, Austerlitz regards the items in the display window of a resale shop as if he were viewing still life paintings, and he asks himself, "What was the meaning" of this object? "What secret lay behind" that one?[44] Knowing that some of these things once belonged to victims of the war, he regards them as evidence. The things bear witness to lost lives but offer no explanation and draw no conclusion:

he and Adorno discussed another talk. Adler proposed the title, "The Theresienstadt Film: Human Blindness under Slavery," but Adorno wanted the topic to be "The Theresienstadt Film: Ideologies under Slavery." Jeremy Adler comments, "Presumably Adler wished to discuss the psychological phenomenon of the inmate's self-deception in contributing to a propaganda film in the camp, whilst Adorno wanted to couple this with a specific critique of ideology."

[42] Sebald, *Austerlitz*, 247.

[43] Rick Poynor, "W. G. Sebald: Writing with Pictures," http://designobserver.com/article.php?id=23618, December 21, 2010.

[44] Sebald, *Austerlitz*, 195.

What, I asked myself, said Austerlitz, might be the significance of the river never rising from any source, never flowing out into any sea but always back into itself, what was the meaning of *veverka*, the [stuffed] squirrel forever perched in the same position, or of the ivory-colored porcelain group of a hero on horseback turning to look back…? They were all as timeless as that moment of rescue, perpetuated but forever just occurring, these ornaments, utensils, and mementoes stranded in the Terezín bazaar, objects that for reasons one could never know had outlived their former owners and survived the process of destruction. (196–97)

Some of the random objects in the window form patterns with other elements in the text. For example, the stuffed squirrel causes Austerlitz to remember the Czech word *veverka*,[45] and squirrels are mentioned throughout the text. Vera wonders, "How indeed do the squirrels know, what do we know ourselves, how do we remember, and what is it we find in the end?"[46] After his trip to Prague and Terezín, Austerlitz has a breakdown and is hospitalized in England for a year. As he recovers, he watches squirrels from his hospital window (230). Returning to his research in Paris, he daydreams about "two mythical squirrels" in the courtyard of the *Bibliotheque Nationale* (281). Austerlitz does not discern a meaning in these recurring references to squirrels, but readers might construct multiple patterns.

---

[45] Thomas, *Prague Palimpsest*, 160. Thomas discusses the significance of Austerlitz's remembering the Czech word.

[46] Sebald, *Austerlitz*, 204. See also John Zilcosky, "Lost and Found: Disorientation, Nostalgia, and Holocaust Melodrama in Sebald's *Austerlitz*," *MLN* 121 (2006): 692. He reads this passage as evidence of the "ultimate unrecoverability of history: Austerlitz realizes that he is like a squirrel that has buried its nuts in the fall and cannot find them in the winter."

Austerlitz's visit to the Ghetto Museum in Terezín dramatizes the meaning of things. Viewing display panels, maps, photographs, and objects used by prisoners, Austerlitz finally confronts "the history of the persecution which my avoidance system had kept from me for so long" (198). Lives were lost, but objects were rescued. This is not metonymy or metaphor; the objects neither stand for nor take the place of their owners. These things are not symbols of other objects lost in other wars. The objects live on as particular things, though their owners are dead. Austerlitz asks himself what the significance of this survival might be, but he does not give an answer. The exhibit displays remnants of the past but does not explain it:

> I understood it all now, yet I did not understand it, for every detail that was revealed to me as I went through the museum from room to room and back again, ignorant as I feared I had been through my own fault, far exceeded my comprehension. (199)

Even after he overcomes his willed ignorance of the past, after he returns to his birthplace, he cannot understand. He enacts Sebald's imperative: one must know everything but explain nothing.

Like Grass and Adler, Sebald distrusts representation. It fails to convey the actual experience of violence, yet it imposes meaning on events. Deeply skeptical of victims' testimony as well as historical and aesthetic reconstructions, all three authors place more confidence in things than in narrative, Adler and Grass with regret, Sebald with relief. As *Austerlitz* demonstrates, objects provide evidence that events occurred, if not why they occurred. Nevertheless, to say that the meaning of things is more reliable than the meaning of words is a meaningful statement. It suggests a rhetorical solution to the rhetorical dilemma of twentieth-century writers. Saying that the Holocaust is indescribable describes it; saying it is unrepresentable represents it; saying it is unknowable makes it known. Similarly, when writers attribute agency to things, they say something about people. To speak of the life of things deadens people; to respect the agency of things mocks the woeful inadequacy of human agency; to claim that things remember what we forget indicts us for failing to remember.

Epilogue: The end of the secular age

The terrorist attacks of September 11, 2001, were the first horrific event of the new century, yet the public knew how to respond. As Roger Angell wrote in *The New Yorker* only a few weeks after the attacks:

> There's nothing new about this if you've lived awhile .... We woke up to Hiroshima, Dallas came at lunchtime, and My Lai by slow degrees. Young people have been looking at us lately and saying, "I don't see how you could have done that, gone through so much. It's beyond my imagination," and we think, Kid, there's nothing to it. Just wait and see.[1]

Unlike earlier writers, Angell knows how to deal with the nightmares of history.[2] He absorbs the shock of unimaginable events by proposing parallels to historical antecedents. This is

---

[1] Roger Angell, "Tuesday, and After," *The New Yorker*, September 24, 2001, 30–31.
[2] See also Judith Greenberg, ed., *Trauma at Home: After 9/11* (Lincoln and London: University of Nebraska Press, 2003). This collection of essays expresses a range of responses to 9/11. Several writers emphasize that prior experiences such as personal trauma and movies shaped their reactions.

the twentieth-century strategy that T. S. Eliot theorized as the mythical method in his 1923 essay "*Ulysses*, Order, and Myth" and implemented in *The Waste Land*. It is also the strategy that Galway Kinnell uses to write about 9/11 in "When the Towers Fell," which was published in *The New Yorker* to commemorate the first anniversary of the attacks. Just as Eliot turned to Joyce to find a way to represent the "immense panorama of futility and anarchy which is contemporary history,"[3] Kinnell turned to Eliot to write about the nightmare of 9/11.

"When the Towers Fell" takes its form—but not its meaning—from *The Waste Land*. Kinnell's title exploits a fortuitous parallel between the twin towers of the World Trade Center and the monuments of earlier imperial capitals that Eliot names:

Falling towers
Jerusalem Athens Alexandria
Vienna London
Unreal[4]

Each of these empires seemed invulnerable until it fell, and "Unreal" anticipates the disbelief of the young people who tell Angell that they cannot imagine how he has gone through so much. Numerous verbal echoes between the two poems reinforce the historical parallels. For example, Eliot's "By the waters of Leman I sat down and wept" (42) can be heard behind these lines:

---

[3] Eliot, "*Ulysses*, Order, and Myth," 177.
[4] T. S. Eliot, *The Complete Poems and Plays, 1909–1950* (New York: Harcourt, Brace & World, Inc., 1962, 48.

And I sat down by the waters of the Hudson,

by the North Cove Yacht Harbor, and thought

how those on the high floors must have suffered .... [5]

Eliot's symbolic geography in "Flowed up the hill and down King William Street,/To where Saint Mary Woolnoth kept the hours"[6] leads to these lines:

The plane screamed low down lower Fifth Avenue

lifted at the Arch, someone said, shaking the dog walkers

in Washington Square Park, drove for the north tower .... [7]

Just as Eliot cites other texts, many not in English, Kinnell includes lines from other poems about loss in their original languages. He quotes Whitman as well as François Villon, Paul Celan, and Aleksander Wat. Like Eliot, Kinnell portrays individuals across the social spectrum:

The banker is talking to London.

Humberto is delivering breakfast sandwiches.

The trader is already working the phone.

The mail sorter has started sorting the mail. (53)

These similarities indicate that Kinnell found a formal model for writing about 9/11 in *The Waste Land*.

Where Eliot's range of sources and voices is ironic, however, Kinnell's is sincere. In *The Waste Land*, the incongruous juxtaposition

---

[5] Galway Kinnell, "When the Towers Fell," *The New Yorker*, September 16, 2002, 55.

[6] Eliot, *Complete Poems and Plays*, 39.

[7] Kinnell, "When the Towers Fell," 53.

of characters, quotations, tones, discourses, and images prevents the reader from discerning any consistent point of view. The poem's ironic disparities destabilize meanings. The fragmentary structure of *The Waste Land* reflects the absence of consensus in the secular culture that Charles Taylor delineates. Kinnell's poem, however, is a coherent narrative. In contrast to Eliot's diverse voices, Kinnell's first-person speaker maintains a consistent tone, unifying the disparate elements of the poem. Assuming the role of spokesperson, he begins with the intimate "we" of a couple "at our high window" looking at the towers before the attacks. He withdraws to an individual "I," moves to the public "we" of the city, and then returns to the singular "I."

Published a year after the attacks, Kinnell's poem maintains the sincerity of many early responses. Roger Rosenblatt summed up the new mood in the title of his commentary, "The Age of Irony Comes to an End." Suddenly, feelings seemed "real":

> When the white dust settles, and the bereaved are alone in their houses, there will be nothing but grief around them, and nothing is more real than that. In short, people may at last be ready to say what they wholeheartedly believe. The kindness of people toward others in distress is real. There is nothing to see through in that. Honor and fair play? Real. And the preciousness of ordinary living is real as well—all to be taken seriously, perhaps, in a new and chastened time. The greatness of the country: real. The anger: real. The pain: too real.[8]

---

[8] Roger Rosenblatt, "The Age of Irony Comes to an End," *Time*, September 24, 2001, 79.

Kinnell evokes this pain by dwelling on the victims. He imagines those who died, those who survived, and those who searched for relatives. He attempts to find meaning in these losses by connecting them to other deaths. The search for bodies "always goes on/ somewhere, now in New York and Kabul."[9] This is a factual statement, not a comparison.

Unlike Eliot, Kinnell finds meaning in the violent events he names. He distinguishes his method from a comparison, which would suggest a commonality among atrocities or weigh the relative violence of each one:

> This is not a comparison but a corollary,
> not a likeness but a lineage
> in the twentieth-century history of violent death—(54)

Substituting "corollary" for Eliot's "continuous parallel," Kinnell situates his references to the past in a causal relationship. A "corollary" is a necessary consequence of a previous event, and a "lineage" is a linked sequence. Instead of offering indeterminate narratives, Kinnell identifies causes and consequences:

> Seeing the towers vomit these black omens, that the last century
>   dumped into this one, for us to dispose of, we know
> they are our futures …. (54)

The poem is a statement about the meaning of 9/11. Extending the "lineage" of violence geographically and temporally, Kinnell represents

---

[9] Kinnell, "When the Towers Fell," 54.

the destruction of the World Trade Center as an attack on a polyglot, multicultural, and unified New York City.

The individual figures in "When the Towers Fell" are bound together as victims of the same catastrophe. Whereas Eliot represents a secular culture of competing beliefs, Kinnell speaks for a new community. Lacking irony, Kinnell's poem is an elegy. It mourns a communal loss and speaks for all victims. The poem ends with the elegiac affirmation that the dead survive in us:

> As each tower goes down, it concentrates
> into itself, transforms itself
> infinitely slowly into a black hole
>
> infinitesimally small: mass
> without space, where each light,
> each life, put out, lies down within us. (55)

The black hole is not a void but a dense mass.

At the end of the secular century, Kinnell speaks for a new consensus. "When the Towers Fell" offers far more than the "stony rubbish" and "broken images" of a waste land. In contrast to Eliot's fragments, Kinnell creates a new global fusion from the wreckage of the World Trade Center. In contrast to the indeterminacy of *The Waste Land*, "When the Towers Fell" affirms a meaning. Kinnell's beautiful images of a terrible event condemn the terrorists and commemorate the victims. This is not a hopeful message, but it is a meaning.

More than a decade has passed since Kinnell wrote "When the Towers Fell," and the sense of community that followed 9/11 has disintegrated. Irony has returned. The competing beliefs that Taylor observed at the turn of the nineteenth century are back, again segmenting society. His definition of secularity encompasses the twentieth-century's religious and nonreligious beliefs, as well as the twenty-first century's fundamentalisms and new materialisms. Nevertheless, secularity today is different. In contrast to the earlier "fragilization" of all beliefs, there is now a hardening of convictions. Each faction is certain of its own truth and hostile to everyone else's. As Harari shows, the legacy of Sensationism is that victims of violence trust the truth of their own experience, a truth that is incontrovertible yet incommunicable. This ideology prevents those who have endured extreme violence from accepting anyone else's claims. In our time, communities are based on a bond among victims of the same acts of violence. Survivors believe that they, and only they, know the meaning of their common experience. If violence reveals truth, and if this truth is incommunicable, there is no basis for a wider consensus.

BIBLIOGRAPHY

Achebe, Chinua. "An Image of Africa: Racism in Conrad's *Heart of Darkness*." In *Heart of Darkness*, 4th edn., edited by Paul B. Armstrong, 336–49. New York: Norton, 2006.

Adams, Jenni. *Magic Realism in Holocaust Literature: Troping the Traumatic Real*. Hampshire: Palgrave Macmillan, 2011.

Adler, H. G. *Panorama*. Translated by Peter Filkins. New York: Random House, 2011.

Adler, H. G. *The Wall*. Translated by Peter Filkins. New York: Random House, 2014.

Adler, Jeremy. "Good Against Evil? H. G. Adler, T. W. Adorno and the Representation of the Holocaust." In *The German-Jewish Dilemma from the Enlightenment to the Shoah*, edited by Edward Timms and Andrea Hammel, 255–89. Lewiston: Edwin Mellen Press, 1999.

Adler, Jeremy. "'The World of My Father's Memory Writing: The *Gesamtkunstwerk* of H. G. Adler." In *H. G. Adler: Life, Literature, Legacy*, edited by Julia Creet, Sara R. Horowitz, and Amira Bojadzija-Dan, 23–46. Evanston, IL: Northwestern University Press, 2016.

Adorno, Theodor. "Cultural Criticism and Society." In *Prisms*. Translated by Samuel and Shierrey Weber, 17–34. Cambridge, MA: MIT Press, 1967.

Angell, Roger. "Tuesday, and After." *The New Yorker*, September 24, 2001, 30–31.

Armstrong, Paul B. *Play and the Politics of Reading: The Social Uses of Modernist Form*. Ithaca and London: Cornell University Press, 2005.

Arnold, Matthew. "The Study of Poetry." In *Complete Prose Works of Matthew Arnold, Vol. 9: English Literature and Irish Politics*, edited by R. H. Super, 161–88. Ann Arbor: University of Michigan, 1973.

Attridge, Derek. "Joyce and the Making of Modernism: The Question of Technique." In *Rethinking Modernism*, edited by Marianne Thormählen, 149–59. New York: Palgrave Macmillan, 2003.

Bader, Rudolf. "Indian Tin Drum." *International Fiction Review* 11 (1984): 75–83.

Bartov, Omer. "H. G. Adler and First-Person History." In *H. G. Adler: Life, Literature, Legacy*, edited by Julia Creet, Sara R. Horowitz, and Amira Bojadzija-Dan, 119–37. Evanston, IL: Northwestern University Press, 2016.

Bell-Villada, Gene H. "García Márquez and the Novel." *Latin American Literary Review* 13 (1985): 15–23.

Benn, Gottfried. *Primal Vision: Selected Writings of Gottfried Benn*. Edited
    by E. B. Ashton. New York: New Directions, 1971.
Bonadeo, Alfredo. "War and Degradation: Gleanings from the Literature of the
    Great War." *Comparative Literature Studies* 21 (1984): 409–33.
Boscagli, Maurizia. *Stuff Theory: Everyday Objects, Radical Materialism*. New
    York: Bloomsbury Academic, 2014.
Braham, Persephone. *From Amazons to Zombies: Monsters in Latin America*.
    Lewisburg: Bucknell University Press, 2015.
Brantlinger, Patrick. "Imperialism, Impressionism, and the Politics of Style." In
    Heart of Darkness, 4th edn., edited by Paul B. Armstrong, 386–95. New York:
    W.W. Norton, 2006.
Brown, Bill. *A Sense of Things: The Object Matter of American Literature*.
    Chicago: University of Chicago Press, 2003.
Brown, Bill. "Thing Theory." *Critical Inquiry* 28 (2001): 1–22.
Brown, Russell E. "Time of Day in Early Expressionist Poetry." *PMLA* 84 (1969):
    20–28.
Burke, Edmund. *A Philosophical Enquiry into the Origin of our Ideas of the
    Sublime and Beautiful*, 2nd edn. London: R. & J. Dodsley, 1759. ECCO
    release 11/01/2004.
Carpentier, Alejo. "The Baroque and the Marvelous Real." In *Magical Realism:
    Theory, History, Community*, edited by Lois Parkinson Zamora and Wendy B.
    Faris, 89–108. Durham and London: Duke University Press, 1995a.
Carpentier, Alejo. "On the Marvelous Real in America." In *Magical Realism:
    Theory, History, Community*, edited by Lois Parkinson Zamora and Wendy B.
    Faris, 75–88. Durham and London: Duke University Press, 1995b.
Caruth, Cathy. *Listening to Trauma: Conversations with Leaders in the Theory
    and Treatment of Catastrophic Experience*. Baltimore: Johns Hopkins
    University Press, 2014.
Caruth, Cathy. *Unclaimed Experience: Trauma, Narrative, and History*.
    Baltimore: Johns Hopkins University Press, 1996.
Cobb, Humphrey. *Paths of Glory*. New York: Penguin, 2010.
Cohen, Milton A. "Fatal Symbiosis: Modernism and World War I." *War,
    Literature, and the Arts* 8 (1996): 1–46.
Connell, Liam. "Discarding Magic Realism: Modernism, Anthropology, and
    Critical Practice." *ARIEL* 29 (1998): 95–110.
Conniff, Brian. "The Dark Side of Magical Realism: Science, Oppression, and
    Apocalypse in *One Hundred Years of Solitude*." *Modern Fiction Studies* 36
    (1990): 167–79.
Conrad, Joseph. *Collected Letters of Joseph Conrad*. Vol. 2. Edited by Frederick
    R. Karl and Laurence Davies. Cambridge: Cambridge University Press, 1986.
Conrad, Joseph. *Heart of Darkness*. 4th edn, edited by Paul B. Armstrong. New
    York: W.W. Norton, 2006.

de Mendelssohn, Peter. *S. Fischer und sein Verlag*. Frankfurt am Main: S. Fischer Verlag, 1970.

Demetz, Peter. "Afterword." In *Panorama*, by H. G. Adler, translated by Peter Filkins, 441–50. New York: Random House, 2011.

Dettmar, Kevin J. H. *The Illicit Joyce of Postmodernism: Reading against the Grain*. Madison: University of Wisconsin Press, 1996.

Döblin, Alfred. *Berlin Alexanderplatz: The Story of Franz Biberkopf*. Translated by Eugene Jolas. New York: Frederick Ungar Publishing Co., 1931.

Döblin, Alfred. "'Ulysses' von Joyce." *Das Deutsche Buch* 8 (1928): 84–86.

Dollenmayer, David B. *The Berlin Novels of Alfred Döblin*. Berkeley: University of California Press, 1988.

Donahue, Neil H. "Introduction." In *A Companion to the Literature of German Expressionism*, edited by Neil H. Donahue, 1–35. Rochester, NY: Camden House, 2005.

Duffy, Enda. *The Subaltern "Ulysses."* Minneapolis and London: University of Minnesota Press, 1994.

Durix, Jean-Pierre. *Mimesis, Genres and Post-Colonial Discourse: Deconstructing Magic Realism*. New York: St. Martin's Press, Inc., 1998.

Duttlinger, Carolin. "Traumatic Photographs: Remembrance and the Technical Media in W. G. Sebald's *Austerlitz*." In *W. G. Sebald: A Critical Companion*, edited by J. J. Long and Anne Whitehead, 155–71. Seattle: University of Washington Press, 2004.

Eksteins, Modris. *Rites of Spring: The Great War and the Birth of the Modern Age*. Boston: Houghton Mifflin, 1989.

Elger, Dietmar. *Expressionism: A Revolution in German Art*. Köln: Taschen, 2002.

Eliot, T. S. *The Complete Poems and Plays, 1909–1950*. New York: Harcourt, Brace & World, Inc., 1962.

Eliot, T. S. *Inventions of the March Hare*. Edited by Christopher Ricks. New York: Harcourt Brace & Company, 1996.

Eliot, T. S. *Letters of T. S. Eliot*. Vol. 1. Edited by Valerie Eliot. New York: Harcourt Brace Jovanovich, 1988.

Eliot, T. S. "The Perfect Critic." In *The Sacred Wood*, 1–16. London: Methuen, 1950.

Eliot, T. S. "Tradition and the Individual Talent." In *Selected Essays*, 3–11. New York: Harcourt, Brace & World, Inc., 1964.

Eliot, T. S. "*Ulysses*, Order, and Myth." In *Selected Prose of T. S. Eliot*, edited by Frank Kermode, 175–78. New York: Harcourt Brace Jovanovich, 1975.

Eliot, Valerie, ed. *The Waste Land. A Facsimile and Transcript of the Original Drafts Including the Annotations of Ezra Pound*. New York: Harcourt Brace Javanovich, Inc. 1971.

Faris, Wendy B., trans. "Magic Realism: Post-Expressionism (1925)." In
    Magical Realism: Theory, History, Community, edited by Lois Parkinson
    Zamora and Wendy B. Faris, 15–31. Durham and London: Duke University
    Press, 1995.

Faris, Wendy R. *Ordinary Enchantments: Magical Realism and the
    Remystification of Narrative*. Nashville: Vanderbilt University Press, 2004.

Felman, Shoshana. "Camus' *The Plague*, or a Monument to Witnessing." In
    Testimony: Crises of Witnessing in Literature, Psychoanalysis, and History,
    edited by Shoshana Felman and Dori Laub, M. D., 93–119. New York:
    Routledge, 1992a.

Felman, Shoshana and Dori Laub, M. D. "Foreword." In *Testimony: Crises of
    Witnessing in Literature, Psychoanalysis, and History*, edited by Shoshana
    Felman and Dori Laub, M. D., xiii–xx. New York: Routledge, 1992b.

Felski, Rita. "Latour and Literary Studies." *PMLA* 130 (2015): 737–42.

Filkins, Peter. "Introduction." In *Panorama*, by H. G. Adler, translated by Peter
    Filkins, xi–xxii. New York: Random House, 2011.

Filkins, Peter. "The Self Positioned, The (De)posited Self, The Soul Released:
    The Uses of Biography in H. G. Adler's Shoah Trilogy." In *H. G. Adler:
    Life, Literature, Legacy*, edited by Julia Creet, Sara R. Horowitz, and Amira
    Bojadzija-Dan, 47–67. Evanston, IL: Northwestern University Press, 2016.

Foucault, Michel. *The History of Sexuality*. Vol. 1. Translated by Robert Hurley.
    New York: Pantheon, 1978.

Freud, Sigmund. *Jokes and Their Relation to the Unconscious (1905)*. Standard
    Edition of the Complete Psychological Works of Sigmund Freud. Vol 8.
    Translated and edited by James Strachey. London: Hogarth Press, 1960.

García Márquez, Gabriel. "Dos o tres cosas sobre 'la novela de la violencia.'" In
    De Europa y América, Obra periodística 3 (1955–1960), edited by Jacques
    Gilard, 646–50. Barcelona: Mondadori, 1992.

García Márquez, Gabriel. "Fantasía y creación artística en América Latina y el
    Caribe." *Texto critico* 14 (1979): 3–8.

García Márquez, Gabriel. *Living to Tell the Tale*. Translated by Edith Grossman.
    New York: Alfred A. Knopf, 2003.

García Márquez, Gabriel. *One Hundred Years of Solitude*. Translated by Gregory
    Rabassa. New York: Perennial Classics, 1970.

Gilbert, Stuart. *James Joyce's "Ulysses": A Study*. New York: Vintage, 1952.

Gordon, John. *Joyce and Reality: The Empirical Strikes Back*. Syracuse, New
    York: Syracuse University Press, 2004.

Grass, Günter. *Peeling the Onion*. Translated by Michael Henry Heim. Orlando,
    FL: Harcourt, Inc., 2007.

Grass, Günter. *The Tin Drum*. Translated by Breon Mitchell. Boston and New
    York: Houghton Mifflin Harcourt, 2010.

Grass, Günter. "Über meinen Lehrer Döblin und andere Vorträge." In *Alfred Döblin, 1878–1978*, edited by Jochen Meyer, 519–21. Marbach am Neckar: Deutsche Schillergesellschaft, 1978.

Greenberg, Judith, ed. *Trauma at Home: After 9/11*. Lincoln and London: University of Nebraska Press, 2003.

Guenther, Irene. "Magic Realism, New Objectivity, and the Arts during the Weimar Republic." In *Magical Realism: Theory, History, Community*, edited by Lois Parkinson Zamora and Wendy B. Faris, 33–73. Durham and London: Duke University Press, 1995.

Guibert, Rita. "Gabriel García Márquez." In *Seven Voices: Seven Latin American Writers Talk to Rita Guibert*. Translated by Frances Partridge, 303–37. New York: Alfred A. Knopf, 1973.

Harari, Yuval Noah. "Scholars, Eyewitnesses, and Flesh-Witnesses of War: A Tense Relationship." *Partial Answers* 7 (2009): 213–28.

Harari, Yuval Noah. *The Ultimate Experience: Battlefield Revelations and the Making of Modern War Culture, 1450–2000*. Hampshire: Palgrave Macmillan, 2008.

Harrison, Thomas. *1910: The Emancipation of Dissonance*. Berkeley, Los Angeles and London: University of California Press, 1996.

Hassan, Ihab. "The Literature of Silence." In *The Postmodern Turn: Essays in Postmodern Theory and Culture*, 3–22. Ohio State University Press, 1987a.

Hassan, Ihab. "Pluralism in Postmodern Perspective." In *The Postmodern Turn: Essays in Postmodern Theory and Culture*, 167–87. Ohio State University Press, 1987b.

Herd, E. W. "Tin Drum and Snake-Charmer's Flute: Salman Rushdie's Debt to Günter Grass." *New Comparison* 6 (1988): 205–18.

Hirsch, Marianne. *The Generation of Postmemory: Writing and Visual Culture After the Holocaust*. New York: Columbia University Press, 2012.

Ho, Janice. "The Crisis of Liberalism and the Politics of Modernism." *Literature Compass* 8 (2011): 47–65.

Hofmann, Klaus. "Poetry After Auschwitz—Adorno's Dictum." *German Life and Letters* 58 (2005): 182–94.

Ireland, Kenneth R. "Doing Very Dangerous Things: *Die Blechtrommel* and *Midnight's Children*." *Comparative Literature* 42 (1990): 335–62

Jager, Colin. "Romanticism/Secularization/Secularism." *Literature Compass* 5 (2008): 791–806.

Jakobson, Roman and Morris Halle. *Fundamentals of Language*. The Hague: Mouton de Gruyter, 1956.

Jameson, Fredric. *The Political Unconscious: Narrative as a Socially Symbolic Act*. Ithaca, NY: Cornell University Press, 1981.

Jameson, Fredric. "*Ulysses* in History." In *James Joyce: A Collection of Critical Essays*, edited by Mary T. Reynolds, 145–58. Englewood Cliffs, NJ: Prentice-Hall, 1993.

Jameson, Fredric. "War and Representation." *PMLA* 124 (2009): 1532–47.

Janes, Regina. "Liberals, Conservatives, and Bananas: Colombian Politics in the Fictions of Gabriel García Márquez." In *Gabriel García Márquez*, edited by Harold Bloom, 125–46. New York: Chelsea House, 1989.

Joyce, James. *Ulysses*. Edited by Hans Walter Gabler. New York: Vintage Books, 1986.

Kandinsky, Wassily. *Concerning the Spiritual in Art*. Translated by M. T. H. Sadler. New York: Dover Publications, 1977.

Kiberd, Declan. "James Joyce and Mythic Realism." In *The Regional Novel in Britain and Ireland, 1800–1990*, edited by K. D. M. Snell, 136–63. Cambridge, England: Cambridge University Press, 1998.

Kinkead-Weekes, Mark. *D. H. Lawrence: Triumph to Exile, 1912–1922*. Cambridge: Cambridge University Press, 1996.

Kinkead-Weekes, Mark. "Violence in *Women in Love*." In *D. H. Lawrence's "Women in Love,"* edited by David Ellis, 221–44. Oxford: Oxford University Press, 2006.

Kinnell, Galway. "When the Towers Fell." *The New Yorker*, September 16, 2002, 53–55.

Kortenaar, Neil ten. "Salman Rushdie's Magic Realism and the Return of Inescapable Romance." *University of Toronto Quarterly* 71 (2002): 765–85.

Kortenaar, Neil ten. *Self, Nation, Text in Salman Rushdie's "Midnight's Children."* Montreal & Kingston: McGill-Queen's University Press, 2004.

Krockel, Carl. *D. H. Lawrence and Germany: The Politics of Influence*. Amsterdam and New York: Rodopi, 2007.

Kubin, Alfred. *The Other Side*. Translated by Mike Mitchell. UK: Dedalus Ltd, 2000.

LaCapra, Dominick. "Writing History, Writing Trauma." In *Writing and Revising the Disciplines*, edited by Jonathan Monroe, 147–80. Ithaca, NY: Cornell University Press, 2002.

Latour, Bruno. "On actor-network theory. A few clarifications plus more than a few complications." *Soziale Welt* 47 (1996): 369–81. http://www.bruno-latour.fr/sites/default/files/P-67%20ACTOR-NETWORK.pdf (accessed June 20, 2016).

Laub, Dori M. D. "An Event Without a Witness: Truth, Testimony and Survival." In *Testimony: Crises of Witnessing in Literature, Psychoanalysis, and History*, edited by Shoshana Felman and Dori Laub, M.D., 75–92. New York: Routledge, 1992.

Lawrence, D. H. "Christs in the Tyrol." In *Twilight in Italy and Other Essays*, edited by Paul Eggert, 43–47. Cambridge: Cambridge University Press, 1994.

Lawrence, D. H. *The First 'Women in Love.'* Edited by John Worthen and Lindeth Vasey. Cambridge: Cambridge University Press, 1998.

Lawrence, D. H. *Letters of D. H. Lawrence.* Vol. 2. Edited by George J. Zytaruk and James T. Boulton. Cambridge: Cambridge University Press, 1981. Vol. 3. Edited by James T. Boulton and Andrew Robertson. Cambridge: Cambridge University Press, 1984.

Lawrence, D. H. *Women in Love.* Edited by David Farmer, Lindeth Vasey, and John Worthen. Cambridge: Cambridge University Press, 1987.

Lawrence, Karen. *The Odyssey of Style in "Ulysses."* Princeton, NJ: Princeton University Press, 1981.

Levenson, Michael. *A Genealogy of Modernism: A Study of English Literary Doctrine, 1908–1922.* Cambridge: Cambridge University Press, 1984.

Levenson, Michael. *Modernism.* New Haven: Yale University Press, 2011.

Levitt, Morton B. *Modernist Survivors.* Columbus: Ohio State University Press, 1987.

Lewis, Beth Irwin. "George Grosz: *Man and Wife*, 1926." In *German Realism of the Twenties: The Artist as Social Critic*, edited by Louise Lincoln, 127. Minneapolis: Minneapolis Institute of Arts, 1980.

Lewis, Pericles. *Religious Experience and the Modernist Novel.* Cambridge: Cambridge University Press, 2010.

Leys, Ruth. *Trauma: A Genealogy.* Chicago: University of Chicago Press, 2000.

Lodge, David. *The Modes of Modern Writing.* Ithaca, NY: Cornell University Press, 1977.

Maddox, Brenda. *D. H. Lawrence: The Story of a Marriage.* New York: Simon and Schuster, 1994.

Marinetti, F. T. "Le Futurisme." *Le Figaro*, February 20, 1909, 1.

Martin, Graham Dunstan. "Introduction." In *Selected Poems: Jules Laforgue*, edited by Graham Dunstan Martin, ix–xxxviii. New York: Penguin, 1998.

Mena, Lucila Inés. "Bibliografía anotada sobre el ciclo de la violencia en la literatura colombiana." *Latin American Research Review* 13 (1978): 95–107.

Menton, Seymour. "Magic Realism: An Annotated International Chronology of the Term." In *Essays in Honor of Frank Dauster*, edited by Kirsten F. Nigro and Sandra M. Cypess, 125–53. Newark, DE: Juan de la Cuesta, 1995.

Menton, Seymour. *Magic Realism Rediscovered, 1918–1981.* Philadelphia: Art Alliance Press and Associated University Presses, 1983.

Merivale, Patricia. "Saleem Fathered by Oskar: *Midnight's Children*, Magic Realism, and *The Tin Drum*." In *Magical Realism: Theory, History, Community*, edited by Lois Parkinson Zamora and Wendy B. Faris, 329–45. Durham and London: Duke University Press, 1995.

Midgley, David. "The Dynamics of Consciousness: Alfred Döblin, *Berlin Alexanderplatz.*" In *The German Novel in the Twentieth Century: Beyond Realism*, edited by David Midgley, 95–109. Edinburgh: Edinburgh University Press, 1993.

Miller, James E. Jr. *T. S. Eliot: The Making of an American Poet, 1888–1922.* University Park, PA: Pennsylvania State University Press, 2005.

Mitchell, Breon. *James Joyce and the German Novel, 1922–1933.* Athens, OH: Ohio University Press, 1976.

Morgan, Peter. "'Your Story is now My Story': The Ethics of Narration in Grass and Sebald." *Monatshefte* 101 (2009): 186–206.

Moses, Michael Valdes. "Magical Realism at World's End." *Literary Imagination: The Review of the Association of Literary Scholars and Critics* 3 (2001): 105–33.

Murphy, Richard. *Theorizing the Avant-Garde: Modernism, Expressionism, and the Problem of Postmodernity.* Cambridge: Cambridge University Press, 1999.

Nash, John. "'Hanging over the bloody paper': Newspapers and Imperialism in *Ulysses.*" In *Modernism and Empire*, edited by Howard J. Booth and Nigel Rigby, 175–96. Manchester and New York: Manchester University Press, 2000.

Nolan, Emer. *James Joyce and Nationalism.* London and New York: Routledge, 1995.

Oates, Joyce Carol. "Lawrence's *Götterdämmerung*: The Tragic Vision of *Women in Love.*" In *D. H. Lawrence's "Women in Love,"* edited by David Ellis, 25–50. Oxford: Oxford University Press, 2006.

Oliva, Achille Bonito. "The Common Sense of the Grotesque." In *George Grosz: The Berlin Years*, edited by Serge Sabarsky, 17–22. New York: Rizzoli International Publications, Inc., 1985.

Pinthus, Kurt, ed. *Menschheitsdämmerung, Dawn of Humanity: A Document of Expressionism.* Translated by Joanna M. Ratych, Ralph Ley, and Robert C. Conard. Columbia, SC: Camden House, 1994.

Pound, Ezra. "A Retrospect." In *Literary Essays of Ezra Pound*, edited by T. S. Eliot, 3–14. New York: New Directions, 1968.

Pound, Ezra. Review of *Prufrock and Other Observations* by T. S. Eliot. *Poetry* 10 (1917): 264–71.

Pound, Ezra. *Selected Letters of Ezra Pound, 1907–1941.* Edited by D. D. Paige. New York: New Directions, 1971.

Pound, Ezra. "Ulysses." In *Literary Essays of Ezra Pound*, edited by T. S. Eliot, 403–09. New York: New Directions, 1968.

Poynar, Rick. "W. G. Sebald: Writing with Pictures." http://designobserver.com/article.php?id=23618 (accessed January 7, 2013).

Presner, Todd Samuel. "'What a Synoptic and Artificial View Reveals': Extreme History and the Modernism of W. G. Sebald's Realism." *Criticism* 46 (2004): 341–60.

Radstone, Susannah. "Trauma Theory: Contexts, Politics, Ethics." *Paragraph* 30 (2007): 9–29.

Rau, Petra. *English Modernism, National Identity and the Germans, 1890–1950.* Surrey, UK: Ashgate Publishing, 2009.

Ricks, Christopher, ed. *Inventions of the March Hare.* New York: Harcourt Brace & Company, 1996.

Rigby, Ida. "Otto Dix, *Self-Portrait with Model,* 1923." In *German Realism of the Twenties: The Artist as Social Critic,* edited by Louise Lincoln, 128. Minneapolis: Minneapolis Institute of Arts, 1980.

Roh, Franz. "Magic Realism: Post-Expressionism (1925)." Translated by Wendy B. Faris. In *Magical Realism: Theory, History, Community,* edited by Lois Parkinson Zamora and Wendy B. Faris, 15–31. Durham and London: Duke University Press, 1995.

Roh, Franz. *Nach-Expressionismus: Magischer Realismus.* Leipzig: Klinkhardt & Biermann, 1925.

Rolleston, James. "Choric Consciousness in Expressionist Poetry: Ernst Stadler, Else Lasker-Schüler, Georg Heym, Georg Trakl, Gottfried Benn." In *A Companion to the Literature of German Expressionism,* edited by Neil H. Donahue, 157–83. Rochester, NY: Camden House, 2005.

Rosenblatt, Roger. "The Age of Irony Comes to an End." *Time,* September 24, 2001, 79.

Rothberg, Michael. *Traumatic Realism: The Demands of Holocaust Representation.* Minneapolis and London: University of Minnesota Press, 2000.

Rushdie, Salman. *Imaginary Homelands.* London: Granta Books, 1991.

Rushdie, Salman. *Midnight's Children.* New York: Random House, 2006.

Sagar, Keith. *D. H. Lawrence's Paintings.* London: Chaucer Press, 2003.

Schmied, Wieland. "Neue Sachlichkeit and German Realism of the Twenties." In *German Realism of the Twenties: The Artist as Social Critic,* edited by Louise Lincoln, 41–56. Minneapolis: Minneapolis Institute of Arts, 1980.

Schultz, H. Stefan. "German Expressionism: 1905–1925." *Chicago Review* 13 (1959): 8–24.

Schvey, Henry. "Lawrence and Expressionism." In *D. H. Lawrence: New Studies,* edited by Christopher Heywood, 124–36. London: Macmillan, 1987.

Schwartz, Frederic J. *The Werkbund: Design Theory and Mass Culture before the First World War.* New Haven and London: Yale University Press, 1996.

Scott, James. "'Continental': The Germanic Dimension of *Women in Love.*" *Literatur in Wissenschaft und Unterricht* 12 (1979): 117–34.

Sebald, W. G. *Austerlitz.* Translated by Anthea Bell. New York: Modern Library, 2001.

Sebald, W. G. "Constructs of Mourning: Günter Grass and Wolfgang Hildesheimer." In *Campo Santo*, translated by Anthea Bell, edited by Sven Meyer, 102–29. London: Penguin, 2006.

Sebald, W. G. *On the Natural History of Destruction.* Translated by Anthea Bell. New York: Random House, 2003.

Seeber, N. U. "D. H. Lawrence, German Expressionism, and Weberian Formal Rationality." *Miscelánea* 20 (1999): 235–57.

Selz, Peter. "The Artist as Social Critic." In *German Realism of the Twenties: The Artist as Social Critic*, edited by Louise Lincoln, 29–40. Minneapolis: Minneapolis Institute of Arts, 1980.

Selz, Peter. *German Expressionist Painting.* Berkeley and Los Angeles: University of California Press, 1957.

Sharp, Francis Michael. "*Menschheitsdämmerung*: The Aging of a Canon." In *A Companion to the Literature of German Expressionism*, edited by Neil H. Donahue, 137–55. Rochester, NY: Camden House, 2005.

Simmons, Alan. "Conrad, Casement, and the Congo Atrocities." In *Heart of Darkness*, 4th edn., edited by Paul B. Armstrong, 181–92. New York: Norton, 2006.

Sokel, Walter H. *The Writer in Extremis: Expressionism in Twentieth-Century German Literature.* Stanford: Stanford University Press, 1959.

Spoo, Robert. "'Nestor' and the Nightmare: The Presence of the Great War in *Ulysses*." In *Joyce and the Subject of History*, edited by Mark A. Wolleager, Victor Luftig, and Robert Spoo, 105–24. Ann Arbor, University of Michigan Press, 1996.

Squires, Michael. "Modernism and the Contours of Violence in D. H. Lawrence's Fiction." *Studies in the Novel* 39 (2007): 84–104.

Stayer, Jayme. "Searching for the Early Eliot: *Inventions of the March Hare*." In *A Companion to T. S. Eliot*, edited by David E. Chinitz, 107–19. Oxford: Wiley-Blackwell, 2009.

Stewart, Jack F. "Expressionism in *The Rainbow*." *Novel* 13 (1980): 296–315.

Surette, Leon. *Dreams of a Totalitarian Utopia: Literary Modernism and Politics.* Montreal: McGill-Queen's University Press, 2011.

Symons, Arthur. *The Symbolist Movement in Literature.* London: Constable, 1908.

Taylor, Charles. *A Secular Age.* Cambridge, MA: Belknap Press of Harvard University Press, 2007.

Thomas, Alfred. *Prague Palimpsest: Writing, Memory, and the City.* Chicago: University of Chicago Press, 2010.

Walcott, Derek. *Collected Poems: 1948-1984*. New York: Farrar, Straus & Giroux, 1986.

Warnes, Christopher. "The Hermeneutics of Vagueness: Magical Realism in Current Literary Critical Discourse." *Journal of Postcolonial Writing* 41 (2005): 1-13.

Warnes, Christopher. "Naturalizing the Supernatural: Faith, Irreverence and Magical Realism." *Literature Compass* 2 (2005): 1-16.

Watt, Ian. *Conrad in the Nineteenth Century*. Berkeley and Los Angeles: University of California Press, 1979.

Weissenberger, Klaus. "Performing the Poem: Rituals of Activism in Expressionist Poetry." In *A Companion to the Literature of German Expressionism*, edited by Neil H. Donahue, 185-228. Rochester, NY: Camden House, 2005.

Wolff, Lynn L. "H. G. Adler and W. G. Sebald: From History and Literature to Literature as Historiography." *Monatshefte* 103 (2011): 257-75.

Woolf, Virginia. "Modern Fiction." In *The Common Reader*, 150-58. New York: Harcourt, Brace & World, 1953.

Worthen, John. "The First '*Women in Love*.'" In *D. H. Lawrence's "Women in Love*," edited by David Ellis, 51-78. Oxford: Oxford University Press, 2006.

Zilcosky, John. "Lost and Found: Disorientation, Nostalgia, and Holocaust Melodrama in Sebald's *Austerlitz*." *MLN* 121 (2006): 679-98.

INDEX

Note: Locators with letter "n" refer to notes.